1986

D1452006

The Public Landscape of the New Deal

Burnham Park, Chicago, shoreline

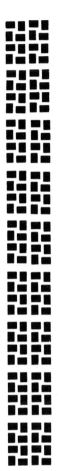

THE
PUBLIC
LANDSCAPE
OF THE
NEW DEAL

Phoebe Cutler

YALE UNIVERSITY PRESS
NEW HAVEN AND LONDON

Designed by James J. Johnson
and set in Goudy Old Style type by
The Composing Room of Michigan, Inc.
Printed in the United States of America by
Vail-Ballou Press, Binghamton, New York.

Library of Congress Cataloging in Publication Data

Cutler, Phoebe, 1947–
    The public landscape of the New Deal.

    Bibliography: p. 167
    Includes index.
    1. Landscape architecture—United States—History—20th century.   2. New Deal, 1933–
1939,   3. United States—Social conditions—1933–1945.   I. Title
SB470.53.C88   1985   333.73′15′0973   85–2437
ISBN 0–300–03256–0

*The paper in this book meets the guidelines for permanence
and durability of the Committee on Production Guidelines
for Book Longevity of the Council on Library Resources.*

10 9 8 7 6 5 4 3 2 1

To
G. C. C., G. C. F., *and* B. C. M.,
who traveled with me.

Contents

Illustrations

Unless otherwise indicated the illustrations are by the author.
Frontispiece Burnham Park, Chicago. Shoreline.

CHARTS

1. Distribution of federal funds affecting profession of landscape architecture and profession of architecture. *(LA)*
2. Federal expenditures, grants, loans and guaranties of loans for construction, 1921–1940. (National Resources Planning Board from Merriam, *Relief and Social Security*)
3. Expenditures for federal grants for non-federal public construction, 1921–1940. (National Resources Planning Board from Lewis Merriam, *Relief and Social Security, 1946*)
4. New Deal ventures in housing.

FIGURES

1. Timberline Lodge, Mt. Hood. (Steve Haugk)
2. Timberline Lodge, Mt. Hood. Bull's head carving. (Madelaine Gill Linden)
3. Site of William E. Sheriden Park, Brooklyn, early 1930s. *(LA)*
4. William E. Sheriden Park, Brooklyn, 1939. *(LA)*
5. Green Brier Park, Chicago. Plan. 1920s. (Weir, *Parks: A Manual of Municipal and County Parks,* Vol. 1, 1928)
6. William E. Sheriden Park, Brooklyn, 1977.
7. Carl Schurz Park, New York. Playground.
8. Marginal Playground #9, Central Park, 1977.
9. Marginal Playground #9, Central Park. Plan. (NYC Dept. of Parks and Recreation)

Acknowledgments

This book began in the gardens of my grandparents. My maternal grandparents no longer lived next door, but the formal garden they had commissioned in 1921 of the New York landscape architect Umberto Innocenti enticed us children. Its pools, terraces, brick steps, and wrought-iron railing conjured up images of a grand and romantic past. On the other side of Boston my paternal grandparents lived in a house the grounds of which the original owner at the outset of the Depression had dedicated to the cause of relieving unemployment. This private WPA project produced a flagstone terrace with lily pool, a rose garden, a set of formal stairs leading down the hill, and, best of all, a mysterious woodland path winding down among trees, crocuses, and rivulets to a woodland pond full of toads. As a young woman gone West I experienced the shock of recognition and longing of nostalgia upon discovering the rose gardens and water chains in Texas and California. Prompted by a bachelor's degree in art history and the need for a topic for a master's in landscape architecture, I started to draw the ties between these childhood and adult landscapes.

As is not uncommon, a graduate thesis evolved into a book, but not without the intercession of a great many people. Foremost among supporters was J. B. Jackson whose own work provided a model for my endeavors. Sound academic criticism and encouragement also came from David Gebhard, Garrett Eckbo, Norman Newton, and Charles Eliot. Mel Scott, Galen Cranz, and Deborah Nevins advised on the particular chapter pertinent to their expertise. From his base at the TVA Technical Library Jesse Mills spurred me on to greater discoveries regarding the TVA and Subsistence Homesteads program. Robert Martensen and Jane Zirpoli Felder contributed invaluable and voluntary editing. Eugene Linden straightened out my thoughts and Elizabeth Jones at Yale tidied them up. Madelaine Gill Linden and Judith Clancy Johns graced the results with beautiful drawings.

Finally any mother of a small child has to thank her progeny for keeping her on a bright-and-early, brief but concentrated work schedule. For the luxury of that schedule I must thank a series of outstanding babysitters on two coasts. Having come to bloom with the help of these people and more, this book ends fittingly in a vernacular mall garden in the Mission district of San Francisco.

Abbreviations

CCC   Civilian Conservation Corps
GPO   United States Government Printing Office
LA   *Landscape Architecture* Magazine
NPS   National Park Service
NRA   National Recreation Association
PWA   Public Works Administration
RDA   Recreation Demonstration Area
TVA   Tennessee Valley Authority
USFS   United States Forest Service
WPA   Works Progress Administration

We are definitely in an era of building; the best kind of building—the building of great public projects for the benefit of the public and with the definite objective of building human happiness.

Franklin Delano Roosevelt

CHAPTER ONE

The New Deal Return to the Land

T EN THOUSAND FEET up the south face of Oregon's Mount Hood the trees halt their climb. The next thousand feet might have remained a bleak moraine, but fifty years ago the Great Depression swept this remote pinnacle like a storm. In its wake it left, not snow and debris, but Timberline Lodge, a wilderness aerie of cut stone, cedar shake, and iron tracery (figs. 1, 2). The joyously emblazoned surfaces of this edifice confirm that for a brief time—1933 to 1942—government merged with artist, craftsman, and conservationist in common purpose and vision.

From this conflation of disparate elements materialized many objects and places of enduring value and appeal. The parks, towers, walls, gardens, lakes, walks, and woods of the Depression are the artifacts of hard times. They are sober, unadorned affairs with little or none of the embellishment of Timberline. These fabrications remaindered from the thirties are poignant reminders that once even the most menial jobs were precious. The Depression outhouse, school building, or picnic shelter testify to humankind's pluck, its grit for survival. The stone furniture, rock pylons, and shake roofs in their dignity and charm illuminate the small scrappy creative core in us all.

Depression artifacts are all around us. Countless roads, picnic grounds, playgrounds, and fifty-foot high trees lining the streets are evidence that for almost a decade following the stock market crash of 1929 this country devoted its energies to the development of the American public landscape. During this interval, known as the New Deal, the administration of Franklin Delano Roosevelt addressed exigencies connected with recreation, forestry, soil conservation, water resources, and housing, at the same time that it was confronting the more familiar crises of unemployment, fiscal turmoil, and industrial malaise.

1. *Timberline Lodge, Mt. Hood.*

2. *Timberline Lodge, bull's head carving.*

Heir to a large estate in the gracious and portentous landscape of the Hudson Valley, Roosevelt was eminently suited to command this immense revitalization of the nation's resources. By the mid-1800s the Hudson Valley was already a flourishing agricultural domain that had inspired the country's first landscape painters and earliest landscape architects. From early childhood Roosevelt occupied himself with the natural lore and the husbandry of his home territory. By the age of twenty-five he was buying property in order to experiment with farming and forestry, including a plan for planting eight thousand trees. While Governor of New York, he purchased property at Warm Springs in the Appalachian hills of Georgia, which exposed him to the vicissitudes of a totally different landscape—one of destitution. There on the slopes of denuded Pine Mountain Roosevelt tried to launch a model farm. As President, Roosevelt, was acting upon his lifelong absorption with the cultivation and care of the land when in 1933 he initiated the land development and regeneration blitz of the New Deal.[1]

Roosevelt's extension past the Hudson and the Appalachians into land renewal and development on a national scale promoted an extraordinary expansion of public facilities. The New Deal land reform transformed areas as diverse as Kansas prairie, California hillside, and Chicago lakefront (frontispiece). The revitalization effort marshalled the abilities of both skilled and unskilled workers. Millions were employed in building recreation and conservation facilities. The very size of the operation led to projects that were overdone, redundant, or merely misguided. As one consequence, the conservation effort of today is often occupied in correcting the conservation work of yesterday. On the other hand, we have inherited a major portion of our public facilities from the federally funded civic industry and natural resource labor of the Depression era.

Ingrained in the traditional land patterns and social mores of the Hudson Valley, Roosevelt did not seek revolutionary change. The buildings and landscapes he engendered reflected the government's essential conservatism. The landscapes derived from venerable European practices transmitted through the pastoral park and the American country estate. Pioneer and Colonial heritage, as well as previous experiments in municipal park and parkway development, also colored Depression-era public work. Avant-garde streamlining occasionally infiltrated, but the extremely limited scope of the *art moderne* influence corroborates the reactionary nature of much of the visible legacy of this era. Where a radical consciousness did surface, it expressed itself more in optimistic dreams than in tangible form. Only fleetingly did collectivistic fervor in Washington succeed in inducing inhabitants in the new federally sponsored settlements to farm jointly or to run cooperative industries. The TVA failed to realize its vision of a nexus of communitarian villages. Romanticism not radicalism ruled the day.

A cohesive, integrated society was sought, in which land patterns would promote a wholesome combination of work, play, and education. In the 1930s Americans still viewed the landscape, along with church and family, as a force in character formation. Recreation enjoyed the moral hegemony that conservation still retains. This idealism imbued the landscape.

Although the government balked at extreme measures, it did stretch its tentacles into new territory. With the end of the Depression, however, the federal government retreated. From New York to Berkeley playgrounds lost their supervisors, and construction of county and state parks subsided. Nonetheless, like the pathbreaking worker's compensation and pension plans, milestones of land policy survive from this era. The Soil Conservation Service still monitors erosion and guards against abusive land practices. The Tennessee Valley Authority is still underwriting agricultural and energy research and demonstration projects. The federalization of shorefront and historical locations that began during the Depression has expanded. In short, the chain of events triggered by Depression-era public works has definitively shaped the nation's topography.

Until now critical review of the New Deal has focused on the economic and political scene with brief digressions into literature, drama, and the graphic arts. Architecture has been slighted and landscape architecture other than town planning has been altogether ignored. This book will attempt to redress this oversight by demonstrating the pervasive and often powerful ways the Depression inscribed itself upon the landscape.

The emergence of the landscape architect was an accidental but influential result of this period. Called *landscape architect* since the mid-1800s, when the term originated in the Hudson Valley, the designer of outdoor spaces had acted to form a professional society in 1899, only some thirty years prior to the New Deal. During the New Deal this new breed of technician—a composite of gardener, civil engineer, and architect—became indispensible to the reordering of the land. Landscape architecture, which was defined as "the art of arranging ground areas and objects upon them for human use and enjoyment and where the appearance of the result is worthy of consideration," became almost totally beholden to Washington.[2] From the state camps of the Civilian Conservation Corps, from the Division of Suburban Resettlement to the Tennessee Valley, the landscape architect was omnipresent. His plans rejuvenated old parks and created new ones.[3] As befitted the collective spirit of the day, no one landscape architect stands out, but as a group the profession proved to be to the United States of the 1930s what Daniel Burnham was to Chicago and Frederick Law Olmsted was to Boston thirty and fifty years before.

In 1935 the American Society of Landscape Architects compiled a chart diagramming the array of agencies active in the federal emergency works program (chart 1). This book will discuss five of these organizations that originated in the Depression and two that predated it. The five are the Works Progress Administration (WPA), the Civilian Conservation Corps (CCC, identified on the chart as "ECW," or Emergency Conservation Work, its original name), the Tennessee Valley Authority (TVA), the Soil Conservation Service, and finally the Resettlement Administration in its various stages. The two organizations that existed before the Depression are the National Park Service (NPS) and the United States Forest Service (USFS). Two other agencies—the National Resources Committee and the Public Works Administration (PWA)—were also influential. Acting in concert, for a few years these agencies greatly accelerated the domestication of the American landscape.

All these organizations participated vigorously in allaying the crises that faced the nation. The most serious problem was, of course, unemployment. When Roosevelt took office 25 percent of the labor force were without jobs. A second urgent dilemma of mass vagrancy grew from the joblessness—the unemployed and partially employed found themselves with a great deal of time on their hands—but was compounded by the lack of recreational facilities. Suspended over these problems was a pervasive fear of widespread lawlessness. Then, along with financial and spiritual destitution, the New Deal administration also confronted the destitution of the land. For several generations careless farmers and foresters had been abusing their heritage. By the 1930s the despoilage had hit home. Blinding dust storms, floods, and rampant erosion finally compelled the nation to act.

Bestirred, the country marshalled two great armies. The first of the

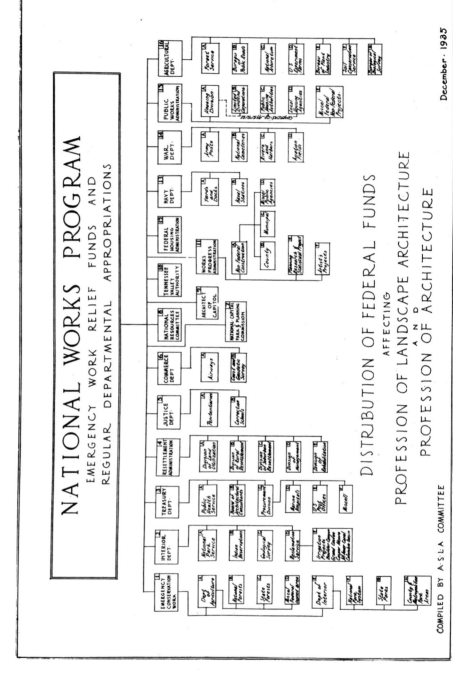

NATIONAL WORKS PROGRAM

EMERGENCY WORK RELIEF FUNDS AND
REGULAR DEPARTMENTAL APPROPRIATIONS

December · 1935

COMPILED BY A·S·L·A COMMITTEE

DISTRIBUTION OF FEDERAL FUNDS
AFFECTING
PROFESSION OF LANDSCAPE ARCHITECTURE
AND
PROFESSION OF ARCHITECTURE

Chart I

two—the Civilian Conservation Corps—was truly a peacetime army. Its recruits, single men ranging in age from 17 to 28, dressed in Army garb, lived in barracks, ate in mess halls, rose at six, and closed the day with a "retreat flag ceremony." This routine lasted throughout the nine-year life of the CCC, from 1933 to 1942. In 1935 500,000 men in over 2,600 camps observed the rigors of this life.[4] The Civilian Conservation Corps was the most popular of the New Deal congeries.

The second army was much vaster and greater in its effect. A sprawling, brawling operation that from 1935 to 1943 employed some eight million people, the Works Progress Administration engaged in projects as diverse as sewing, drama, play supervision, and road construction. With large budgets, little overview, and great ambitions, it was a flawed but gallant combatant. Unlike the Public Works Administration, with which it is often confused, the WPA not only financed eventually up to 80 percent of the cost of its projects, but hired, fired, secured materials, and supervised. Officially the WPA focused on low-cost, short-term jobs that employed large numbers of workers and did not exceed a ceiling of $25,000, but a host of behemoth projects like Timberline, the canals of San Antonio, and the San Francisco Zoo made a mockery out of these ostensible limitations. This insouciance in face of officialdom comprised both the strength and the weakness of the Works Progress Administration.

These two great assemblages of the young, the old, and the unskilled made possible the success of the five remaining organizations pertinent to this book. For the Soil Conservation Service and its affiliate, the Prairie States Forestry Project, the CCC and the WPA collected seeds, tilled nurseries, and planted trees for the giant shelterbelt that was to stay the winds on the back of the Great Plains. For the National Park Service and the U.S. Forest Service they laid roads, cleared trails, strung wires, and built campsites that contributed to the taming of the American landscape. For the Resettlement Administration and Tennessee Valley Authority, the gainfully unemployed graded the land, prepared the foundations, and erected the buildings that realized the New Deal utopia. These agencies' projects helped the New Deal make a boon out of a bust, converting a handicap into an advantage by directing the desperate and discouraged against a lack of public facilities and a blight in the land.

CHAPTER TWO

The New Deal and the New Play

ALTHOUGH NOT ITSELF EXTREME, the government operated against a backdrop of rabid unrest, as turmoil spurred an onslaught of demagogues preaching their personal cures. Louisiana's mercurial governor and senator Huey Long called for a guaranteed income as part of his "Share the Wealth" plan. Broadcasting to the nation from Detroit, Father Coughlin used his "Golden Hour of the Little Flower" radio show to demand the nationalization of all banks. Anarchists like the exiled Emma Goldman were rare; communism, however, culled favor among artists and intellectuals like novelist Theodore Dreiser and critic Edmund Wilson. Historians and the media have embraced the revolutionary rumblings of the Depression and pre-Depression era, but the quieter and less colorful recreation movement has received but scant attention. Piloted in the 1930s by Jesse Steiner, Robert Moses, and George Butler and the National Recreation Association, the movement compelled greater and more effective response than any of the more revolutionary or radical propositions. Ironically, in its response to the recreation movement, Washington unwittingly moved in the direction desired by its radical critics. The Roosevelt administration did not nationalize any banks or equalize income, but it did for almost a decade federalize public recreation development.

In the fall of 1933, sociologist Jesse F. Steiner published in *The New York Times Magazine* an article entitled "The Challenge of the New Leisure." Steiner urged the new government in Washington to apply emergency relief money toward a program of extensive construction and planning in recreation. Previously, federal funding of recreation had been niggardly, at most a few dollars for the national parks. Washington first exhibited an interest in the subject in 1924 when Coolidge convened a National Conference on Outdoor Recreation. This conference legitimized the recreation movement and provoked the publication, in 1928, of L. H. Weir's *Parks: A Manual of Municipal and County Parks* which, along with the prolific work of George D. Butler, shaped the direction of recreation for many years to come.

The movement gained more credence a few years later when Hoover pronounced that "this civilization is not going to depend so much on what we do when we work as what we do in our time off." Hoover appointed a "Council for Research on Social Trends" which undertook the first federally funded social study. Jesse F. Steiner was one of the members of this council. His article in *The New York Times Magazine* in effect popularized the Council's findings on recreation.[1]

The main force behind the sudden interest was the National Recreation Association, which since its inception in 1906 had been vigorously promoting the cause of recreation. It sponsored the 1924 conference, Weir's parks manual, and all the major literature on the subject for the next thirty years. As the editor of the NRA's principal publications, George D. Butler has exerted more influence on modern urban recreation than has any other individual.[2]

First published in 1940, Butler's primer *Introduction to Community Recreation* recapitulates the recreation movement of the thirties, catalogues the causes, and outlines the course of development. As causes Butler lists the growth of cities, the shortened work week, the rise of the automobile and elimination of the street as a safe play area, the surge in unemployment, a trend toward having fewer children, which reduced household tasks, and finally an increase in the number of retired people.

In his summary Butler emphasizes the need for space for structured play. "It is gradually becoming recognized by planning authorities that approximately one half of a city's total park and recreation acreage should be developed for active uses." This statement reflects the character of most of the urban park work done during the Depression.[3] Development prior to the thirties had been concentrated on expansive "pleasure grounds" where the aim of reproducing within the city a slice of the country outweighed the importance of providing a suitable space for games. In the archetypal Central Park in New York and Prospect Park in Brooklyn, provision was made for observing sheep and paddling boats, but only temporary or informal accommodations allowed for tennis, football, or golf. Frederick Law Olmsted and Calvert Vaugh laid out parade grounds, leafy walks, riding trails, and belvederes before basketball courts or children's playgrounds had evolved. But these genteel bucolic settings simply could not fill all the recreation needs of the leisure-rich twentieth century. The WPA attempted to eliminate the leisure gap by building not bandstands and belvederes, but grandstands and athletic fields.[4]

Two charts compiled by the National Resources Committee reveal the extent of the New Deal incursion into recreation. Starting at almost zero, spending in this area exploded—at the local level only road work took a larger share of the total expenditure on construction. Recreation also amassed the third greatest sum of federal money out of fourteen different categories of building (charts 2, 3).

This deluge of money transformed urban topography across the nation. Eastern and midwestern cities expanded and elaborated upon their park systems. Philadelphia developed the thousand-acre Wissahickon section of its focal nineteenth-century Fairmount Park and created a recreational bonanza in League Island, which was promptly rechristened Franklin Delano Park (a name that would soon become commonplace on the nation's maps). New York converted Randall's Island to the same leisure cause and tripled the number of playgrounds across the city. San Francisco doubled its inventory of finished parks. Chicago, which had pioneered playground development, undertook the rehabilitation of 117 small parks. Milwaukee, New York, and Chicago consolidated their fragmented park departments the better to catch the wave. Only in Boston, where the WPA wallowed in politics and chicanery, did the New Deal riches fail to raise a surf.

The New Deal effect in eastern and midwestern cities (other than New York) was modest compared to the revolution wrought in the burgeoning city of Dallas. Prior to the 1930s, Dallas had only a skeletal park system, prepared by landscape architect George Kessler. In consortium with Hare and Hare, a landscape firm out of Kansas City, the WPA breathed life into the bare bones of Lee, Revershon, and White Rock Parks. Consequently, whereas the core of the park systems of more venerable cities is often an Olmsted or pseudo-

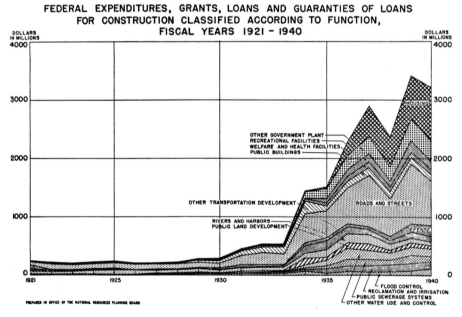

FEDERAL EXPENDITURES, GRANTS, LOANS AND GUARANTIES OF LOANS
FOR CONSTRUCTION CLASSIFIED ACCORDING TO FUNCTION,
FISCAL YEARS 1921 – 1940

Chart 2

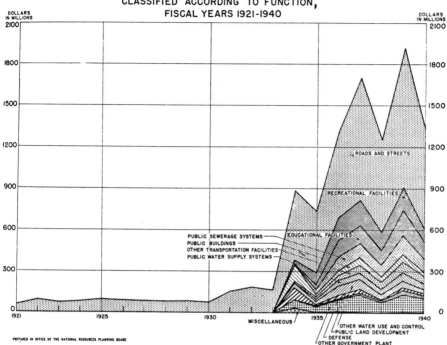

EXPENDITURES FOR FEDERAL GRANTS FOR NON-FEDERAL PUBLIC CONSTRUCTION
CLASSIFIED ACCORDING TO FUNCTION,
FISCAL YEARS 1921-1940

Chart 3

Olmsted pastoral park, in Dallas the New Deal "Beaux Arts" park forms the heart of the system.

But for variety and quantity of recreational space, no city could touch New York. Of course, with a population of almost eight million, almost twice that of Chicago, the second largest city, New York required the most recreation outlets. By 1936 New York City had absorbed one-seventh of all WPA expenditures. Only Montana received a larger per capita share of Washington's bounty. In New York, Parks commissioner Robert Moses assembled a massive force of designers, draftsmen, and engineers—eighteen hundred strong—and cajoled the New Deal administration into footing the bill.[5]

The creations of this professional emergency task force ranged from Bryant Park, the stately, tree-ringed companion to the New York Public Library, to the William E. Sheriden Park in Brooklyn, a standard game field. Such was the range of facilities that in New York the term *playground* still specified a tot lot, whereas elsewhere it signified anything from a children's play space to a neighborhood park. New York was a leader in recreation, as in other areas of design, a magnification of a trend that occurred in cities all over the nation.

The story of the evolution of the William E. Sheriden Park in Brooklyn reveals several aspects of the parks and recreation charette of the thirties.

3. *Site of William E. Sheriden Park, Brooklyn, early 1930s.*

4. *William E. Sheriden Park, Brooklyn, 1939.*

When the park opened, it had been transformed from a dusty vacant lot to a dignified recreation area (figs. 3, 4). The elements and their disposition conformed to practices of the past decade. A plan completed in the 1920s for a Chicago park that was featured in Weir's manual may well have directly inspired the Brooklyn creation (fig. 5). Both parks include a shelter with flagpole and entry court, a court-game inset, and ironmonger equipment arranged around an ample free-play area. The regularity and exacting symmetry place both compositions in the Beaux Arts phase of playground and small park development. *Beaux Arts* refers to nineteenth-century French academic evocation of classic Greek and Roman design. When translated to American playgrounds it describes a very orderly and geometric presentation with all elements carefully balanced.

The landscaping establishment heralded the Sheriden Park as a model of neighborhood park design. The park's subsequent fate was less fortuitous (fig. 6). These vintage 1930s recreation spaces, with their hard lines and surfaces and considered symmetry, need careful attention if they are to age gracefully. Stuck in a sinking lower-middle-class neighborhood, the Sheriden Park could little hope for such care.

Not visible in any picture or plan but perhaps the most crucial factor in the park's decline is the loss of the playground supervisor, an integral part of the Depression era playground.[6] Even at its apex, the park was lean; now it is almost a void. Yet the need for recreational area still remains, and life still ebbs and flows in this raggle-taggle space that has come almost full circle—from vacant lot to empty park.

The Sheriden Park typifies, not only for New York, but also for other cities, the shape of the recreation enthusiasm of the Depression. This basic form appears in both elaborate and stark guises. The playground area in New York's Carl Schurz Park, adjacent to the Mayor's residence and the Park Commissioner's apartment, demonstrates the extent to which the scheme could be dressed up (fig. 7). Cobblestone aprons accent the trees in the standard arrangement. Benches ring the perimeter and face each other in pairs under each tree. The fence is wrought iron, not steel; the comfort station is made of stone, not brick. A swirling, colorful mosaic relieves the drabness of the asphalt and defines the "free play area." Generous space permits screening and separation of the basketball courts, but the core arrangement of a duplicate line of swings, slides, and sandpits remains. This same format appears in reduced form in Riverside, an older, bucolic-style park along the city's western edge where three play areas materialized in the 1930s. Twenty small-scale playgrounds penetrated the rustic splendor of Central Park (figs. 8, 9). These Depression-vintage playgrounds today form an indelible part of the New York cityscape which the process of renovation has only recently begun to transform.[7]

The William E. Sheriden Park and Carl Schurz playground took their

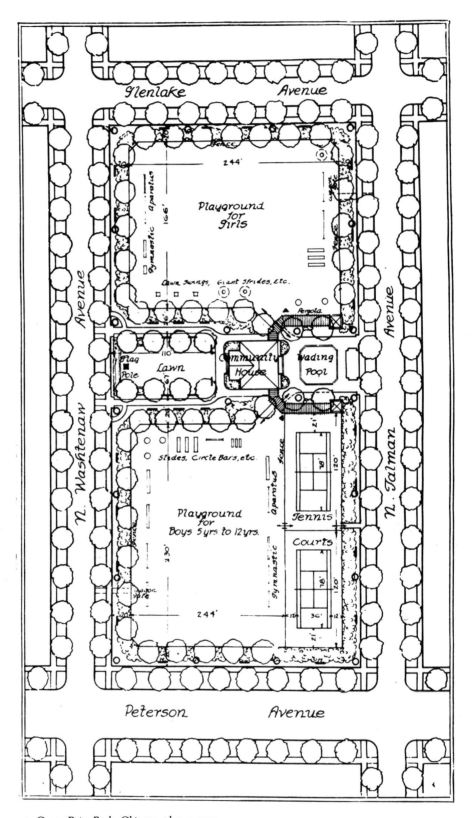

5. *Green Brier Park, Chicago, plan, 1920s.*

form from the code evolved over three decades by the National Recreation Association. Foster and Avalon, matching parks installed in the thirties in Chicago's South Side play back almost verbatim the NRA list of components for a "neighborhood playground." They each contain a centralized shelter house, tennis courts, wading pools, athletic fields, running tracks, tot lots and free play areas (fig. 10). Of the items on the list they lack only a jumping pit. But despite this bounty, Avalon and Foster still lack the finesse that distinguishes Carl Schurz Park. The Chicago parks, like Sheriden, typify a rote response to demand which exceeded the availability of talented designers and, moreover, did not especially value them. Social issues overrode aesthetic concerns in inner-city park design during the Beaux Arts phase.

The New Deal traits of utility, standardization, and austerity penetrated to West Coast parks as well. However, in San Francisco the precipitous terrain enforced a degree of clarification missing from Chicago's and most of New

6. *William E. Sheriden Park, Brooklyn, 1977.*

7. *Carl Schurz Park, New York, playground.*

York's efforts. Playgrounds like Portrero Hill offer the usual sports and a small children's play lot, but terracing divides the activities in an agreeable and sometimes even striking way (fig. 11). Still, the citywide motifs of stucco comfort stations, concrete-edged sandpits, ironmonger play equipment, and curvaceous concrete curbing, coupled with the inevitable basketball, tennis, and baseball areas betrays the prevalence of the engineer mentality mass production ethos of the day. San Francisco, like Chicago and New York, capitalized on the urgency of the socioeconomic situation to produce quantity to the detriment of quality.

Speed was crucial. A capricious Congress ruled over the WPA treasury, and for nine long years every park and city official was working against the expectation that the next year the trove would vanish. This uncertainty did not promote design of lasting dignity. The scenario of boom-and-bust creation in New York went something like this: out of the 1,800-strong design and drafting force, a junior member was assigned to prepare a plan for an empty, irregular lot, roughly ninety by one hundred feet, in the South Bronx. The elements of the design derived ultimately from NRA standards and force of habit. Standards and practice reduced to essentials, the plan was finished in a day or two. A single strand of benches and a double line of trees enclosed a matching set of swings and seesaws with a free play area in between, a comfort station at one end, and a large-scale set of swings at the other. Thus, James C. Lyons Park circa 1935 typifies ready-made, bargain-basement recreation in New York.

Lyons Park, now in one of the most dangerous neighborhoods in the city, was redesigned in 1976. It took one year and twenty-two sheets of drawings to get the plan ready. Two basketball courts, three adjacent back-

8. *Marginal Playground #9, Central Park, 1977.*

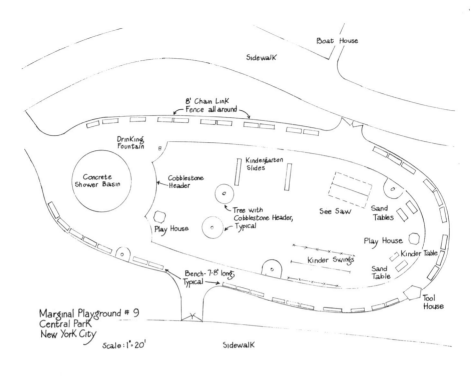

Boat House

Sidewalk

8' Chain Link
Fence all around

Drinking
Fountain

B

Kindergarten
Slides

Concrete
Shower Basin

Cobblestone
Header

Tree with
Cobblestone Header,
Typical

See Saw

Sand
Tables

Play House

Play House

Kinder Table

Kinder Swings

Sand
Table

Sand
Table

Bench- 7-8' long
Typical

Tool
House

Marginal Playground # 9
Central Park
New York City

Scale: 1"=20'

Sidewalk

9. Marginal Playground #9, Central Park, plan.

10. Avalon Park, Chicago, baseball field.

11. *Portrero Hill Playground, San Francisco.*

stops, three surface games, a small children's area with play fountain (a wading pool with water jets), sandbox, and a versatile timber structure, and four surfaces of a grass/stone combination, concrete pavers, granite block, and asphalt replace three sets of swings, two seesaws, a slide, and asphalt. The playground has become aesthetic.

The sobriety and spareness of the Depression play space, as seen in Lyons, Sheriden, Avalon, and Foster Parks, reflects the political and economic expedience of mass production, but even more the didactic mission assigned to the form. The playground was meant to enhance the child, not the environment. The era romanticizes not the place, but the purpose of the place. Before, during, and well after the Depression people equated recreation with character formation. In San Francisco a thirties newsletter funded by the WPA measured the success of a playground not by the quantities of children it attracted, but by the number of nurses, doctors, and lawyers who graduated from its swings.

The WPA-documented tale of a boys' clubhouse in North Little Rock, Arkansas conveys the moralistic fervor attached to the recreation cause. In the first of a series of four photographs, a couple of boys blissfully rummage through a junkyard, so absorbed in their hunt that they take no notice of the WPA photographer indicting them for posterity (fig. 12). The official caption clucks, "Boys at play in a junkyard, illustrative of what youngsters did before

12. Junkyard, Little Rock, Arkansas, 1930s.

13. WPA-built clubhouse, Little Rock, Arkansas, 1930s.

the construction by the WPA of the Boys Club House at North Little Rock."
A second shot, accompanied by a warning of the evils attendant upon uncontrolled excess leisure, captures the boys about to break into a tool shed. The last two photos in the tableau contrast the proud new clubhouse, a substantial rock structure, with the original building, a whimsical wooden shack complete with boys lolling contentedly, or, in New Deal parlance, ominously, on the front porch (figs. 13, 14). The New Deal was concerned with the problem of lack of employment at all levels.

By the end of the decade the aesthetic bleakness perpetrated by the heady combination of didacticism and expedience had become apparent. In 1928 George Butler's *Play Areas* glossed over aesthetic concerns with the casual apology that the necessity of a level, open space afforded "not as much opportunity for introducing an interest element." Ten years later, in *New Play Areas*, Butler declaimed that children naturally love beauty and will bypass a barren area to play in an attractive one. He emphatically pronounced that "there is no justification for failing to include provision for [landscaping]."[8]

If parks were measured by number, zoos and botanical gardens were calibrated by grandeur and finesse. The detailing held back from the playground was lavished on zoos and botanical gardens. Here whimsey and horticultural ornament tempered sobriety, while the inherent education purpose

14. *Former clubhouse, Little Rock, Arkansas, 1930s.*

of zoological and horticultural settings completed the era's zeal for order and instruction. The advent of the New Deal coincided with the trend toward natural, open venues guarded by moats instead of by bars. The impact of the WPA on American zoos (it built at least seventeen of ninety) is epitomized by the gargantuan rock piles dubbed "monkey islands," the best examples of which may be viewed at the Cincinnati, Detroit, and San Francisco zoos. (fig. 15). Complicated ventures involving the application of cement to a multifaceted armature, these zoological follies occupied both architects and large numbers of the unemployed. The idealistic attitude toward public recreation subsidized by a surplus of labor gave the zoos in Central Park, San Diego, Dallas, and Buffalo, in addition to the ones already mentioned, grounds and structures carefully detailed with cascading plants, figurative reliefs, and picturesque bowers for the animals. Botanical gardens, for example those at Berkeley and Cornell, and the Boerner Botanical Gardens of Milwaukee, profited from the same surfeit of attention. In this process of elaboration, a setting for Alpine plants becomes a fairy's lair (fig. 16). The attention to planting and detail that evaded parks surfaced in the favored zoological and botanical gardens, the design of which involved bona fide building and landscape architects, not just civil engineers or hastily assembled draftsmen.

15. *Fleischaaker Zoo, San Francisco, monkey island.*

16. *Boerner Botanical Garden, Milwaukee, rock garden.*

The sobriety of playgrounds in contrast with the lushness of botanical and zoological gardens reflects the gravity with which people regarded children's play. During the Depression era leisure activities were strictly segregated. Tree borders excepted, plants and animals did not mingle with playgrounds. The identities of these developing landscape forms were still too new and fragile to withstand interweaving.

Depression riches and talent rained not only on zoos and botanical gardens but also on the development of aquatic recreation. Although rivers were not favored, lakefronts, seashores, and swimming pools received extensive attention. Beginning in 1937 with the Cape Hatteras National Seashore, a CCC-supported survey of the nation's oceanfront laid the foundation for future nationalization of beaches. The New Deal era expanded the public dominion over littoral land.

The course of aquatic recreation in the thirties and after would have been different without the influence of Robert Moses. A former college swimmer, Moses spent extra time and energy on New York's trend-setting beach and pool extravaganzas. In 1929 he masterminded the magnificent Jones Beach complex, which made instant landscape history. With New Deal assistance, Moses then refurbished and expanded Rockaway Beach and created Orchard Beach (fig. 17). After connecting three islands and a neck and finishing them with sand imported from forty miles away, Moses built a bathhouse complete with a colonnade, a gleaming restaurant, and a prom-

17. Orchard Beach, Bronx.

enade behind which spread a picnic and games area with tennis and handball courts. For those who couldn't make it to the beach or who preferred fresh water, this Caesar among park directors dotted the city with ten magnificent swimming pools. The Astoria Park pool in Queens, the largest, was built to accommodate six thousand people (fig. 18). With a fine view of the Triborough Bridge, this celebrated pool includes bleachers, a long spacious bathhouse, a high diving board, and adjoining it, a large circular spray pool. The "colored pool" inserted into Colonial Park in Harlem vaunts a grandiose brick bathhouse resembling a Medieval fortress. The pool converts into a skating rink in the winter.

Architectural magazines and Moses' reports spread news of New York's achievements across the country. Less elaborate provincial counterparts of New York's pool and shoreline construction sprang up all over. No other waterfront enterprise could match the size and elaboration of Jones or Orchard Beach, but the regional efforts sported a more modern format. In Chicago, Milwaukee, and San Francisco, streamlined bathhouses with porthole windows exemplified the excitement of this new territory in public recreation (fig. 19). The look in leisure architecture generally oscillated from the spare engineered guise of the playground/athletic field to the nostalgia and romance of the Italianate garden or rustic woodland retreat, but the Aquatic Park bathhouse in San Francisco is a rare example of the application of modern forms to the recreation movement of the thirties.

18. *Astoria Pool, Queens.*

19. *Aquatic Park, San Francisco.*

The popularity of pool and shoreline construction shows how far afield—literally to the water's edge—the leisure landscape was spreading. In the Midwest, Milwaukee arrayed itself with a maritime bathhouse at Bradford Beach and six substantial pools, one of which, in McGovern Park, is a graceful, curving deviation from the race-course rectangularity of its New York exemplar (fig. 20). As far away as Raleigh, North Carolina; Kearney, Nebraska; and Stearns, Kentucky; WPA crews were producing pools and bathhouses. The odd juxtaposition of a kidney-shaped swimming pool and what looks like a refurbished log cabin in Stearns, Kentucky does indicate, however, how tentative was the rural extension of the largely urban obsession with organized recreation (fig. 21).

Like the construction of playgrounds, which, although often drab, at least initiated a cycle of recreation development, the aquatic enterprises were a mixed blessing. The shorelines, as demonstrated by the rigidity of the Lake Pontchartrain project, were like the parks and playgrounds fashioned in the government's own solemn image—immutable and hierarchic (fig. 22). At Lake Pontchartrain a categorical design divides boating and promenading. The straight, uncompromising lines of vegetation and circulation declare that recreation is a sober business. In San Francisco concrete banks of waterfront seating defy relaxation, while the announcer's stand alone is a self-contained mini-monument. Bold and tenacious, these aquatic borders offer an uncomplicated welcome to the water's edge. At their best, epitomized by the marine

20. McGovern Park, Milwaukee, swimming pool.

21. *Stearns, Kentucky. Swimming pool, ca. 1935.*

murals, the sinuous announcer's stand, and orderly beds of flowers of San Francisco's Aquatic Park; the clock tower, sweeping colonnade, boundless tile mall, and luxuriant trees of New York's Orchard Beach; or the dignified stone embankment at Chicago's Burnham Park (frontispiece), the artistry of these instantaneous public works amply compensates for their lack of heterogeneity.

Besides offering aesthetic satisfaction, a well-conceived public facility is also more versatile than a poorly planned one. The country is littered with defunct WPA-made recreation buildings, but the great bathhouses still serve a function. When swimming in the cold and periodically polluted waters of San Francisco Bay failed to fire the public imagination, the Aquatic Park bathhouse became a maritime museum and a senior citizens' center. In New York City, the building accompanying the John Jay Swimming Pool has also become a meeting place for the aging generation that built it. The strong designs of these bathhouses have survived the "freakish change of style" that Moses foresaw and the corrosive effect of time that has been detrimental to so much of the Depression landscape.

A good part of the Depression landscape work addressed the threatening gap between leisure time and the availability of recreational facilities. People saw adequate recreational space as vital to the smooth functioning of civilization. The great number of unemployed helped build the needed facilities.

22. *Lake Pontchartrain Aquatic Park, Louisiana.*

Cities competed with each other in an effort to turn out the most parks in the shortest time. The end result, exemplified by New York's William E. Sheridan Park and "Marginal Playground #9" in Central Park, has not always stood the test of time (fig. 8).[9]

In contrast, zoos and botanical gardens offered the building and land-scape architects of the day the ideal opportunity to mesh the two strands—the formal or continental, the informal or the rustic—of their design training and experience. Imposing aquatic parks demonstrate that the recreation cause had also captured the design imagination; the impressive zoological and botanic gardens convey the popular belief in self-betterment through commendatory leisure pursuits. In the 1930s, America began to grapple with a world in which play was becoming equal, if not yet superior, to work.

CHAPTER THREE

The New Deal and the Old World

HE INCREASE IN LEISURE TIME and the influence of Europe led to many fashion fads in the recreation movement. For the first thirty years of the twentieth century Italy dominated fashion in the leisure landscape. Cascades, arbors, and garden theaters swept across the land in tribute to the Mediterranean villa. Typically the flow of ideas and artifacts began in the transmission of Renaissance garden motifs to the estates of the plutocrats and moved from there into the public domain. Although New World designers began by adapting Old World formats, native landscape architects, especially in the Midwest and West, increasingly developed their own indigenous styles which broke from European precedent.

The progression from country estate to city park was a natural one. For years landscape architects had been battening their practices with the embellishment of the country estate, and in the process they compiled a stock of design constructs easily transferable to the public landscape. Cleveland's Cultural Gardens, built on the brow of a hill in Rockefeller Park between 1926 and 1939, looks like a long necklace of gardens that some former estate architect just lifted from past jobs and strung together (fig. 23). At the same time, these twenty units attempted to represent the city's heterogeneous population, with names like "Syrian," "Ukrainian," and some mysterious group called "Rusin." The gardens are an excellent illustration of the adaption of formal European style to the American public landscape. They especially exemplify Italy's strong influence on landscape design. Despite the protestations of numerous patriotic plaques and statues, the recurrent steps, pools, terraces, and walls identify even these flag-waving components as beneficiaries of the Italian Renaissance.

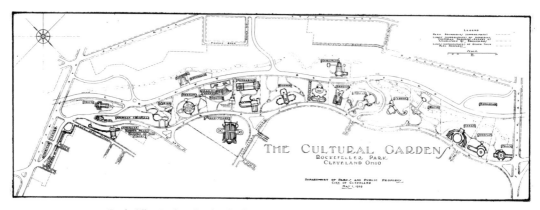

23. Rockefeller Park, Cleveland, plan of Cultural Gardens.

The use of formal architectural style marked a switch in allegiance away from England toward the Continent. American landscape architects proudly acknowledged this new alliance. In 1924 Frank Waugh, head of the University of Massachusetts landscape school, pronounced, "American garden art seems destined to surpass anything ever done before, perhaps even the noble models of the Italian Renaissance."[1] The torrent of arbors, urns, pools, pergolas, and balustrades that emanated from the hillside villas built around Rome, Florence, and Siena between 1400 and 1600 displaced the green swards and tree copses of the English school.

So complete was Italy's ascendance in the first few decades of the twentieth century that American landscape architects spent as much time there as possible. By 1902 the lavish houses and gardens depicted in Guy Lowell's *American Gardens* display the axial lines, classic symmetry, and architectural definition that characterize the high garden art of Renaissance Italy.[2] The familiar details—plentiful pots, statuary, broad steps, pools, and fountains—adorn the exterior design of Stanford White, Carrère and Hastings, and the influential Charles Platt.

In the domain of the formal garden Platt brooked no rival. A New Yorker trained in Paris as an artist, his fascination with Italy impelled him into the practice of architecture and landscape architecture. His 1894 book *Italian Gardens* introduced this country to the landscape practices of the Continent. Platt went on to design a succession of lordly estates in the continental manner between the years 1897 and 1933. So prevalent by the first decade was Platt's Renaissance manner that even Olmsted Brothers, the successor firm to Frederick Law Olmsted and chief heir to the flowing, naturalistic school of English landscape design, succumbed to it. The Olmsted firm (with Arthur Shurcliff) employed every known Italian artifice when creating Castle Hill for plumbing magnate Richard T. Crane in Ipswich, Massachusetts between 1910 and 1918. James Deering, the Chicago industrialist, did not take any chances when he planned for his winter palazzo, Vizcaya, in Miami (fig. 24). He hired a European designer trained in Florence to supply the requisite pools, pergolas, fountains, and parterres that at the turn of the century signified the fullest possible achievement of the American dream.

According to popular belief, somewhere in the whirlwind between the stock market crash of 1929 and Roosevelt's first hundred days, estates like Vizcaya and Castle Hill ceased to be built. Indeed, the chief practitioners of the grand manner—Platt, Ferrucio Vitale, and James Greenleaf—all passed away in 1933. However, neither their passing nor the collapse of the market altogether dispelled the country estate. Between 1931 and 1934 the American Society of Landscape Architects published a four-volume series celebrating the contemporary work of its members. Lavish gardens—although not on the scale of Vizcaya—comprised the majority of the work. Well into the Depression the plan for Seabrook Farms in New Jersey flaunted an array of nine formal gardens (fig. 25).[3]

Two contests reported in the pages of the July 1933 issue of *Landscape Architecture* highlighted the tenacity with which old style and privilege clung on despite economic dysfunction. The competition winner for the prestigious Rome Prize (the prize was a year's fellowship with the American Academy in

24. *Vizcaya, Miami.*

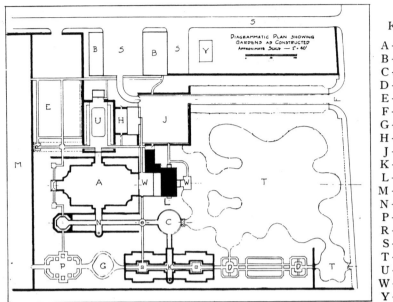

A — Azalea Garden
B — Barns
C — Box Garden
D — Bulb and Annual Garden
E — Cut-flower and Utility Garden
F — Entrance Drive
G — Evergreen Garden
H — Drying Yard
J — Garage Court
K — Holly Garden
L — House
M — Kitchen and Truck Garden
N — Lilac Allée
P — Perennial Garden
R — Rose Borders
S — Service Drive and Courts
T — South Lawn
U — Swimming Pool Garden
W — Terraces
Y — Servant Cottage

25. *Seabrook Farms, New Jersey, diagrammatic plan, 1936.*

Rome) described a restaurant in a grand formal setting with an axial vista radiating far into the distance (fig. 26). The second competition, an intercollegiate one, entailed the planning of a country estate for a man who had lost his money, a condition which had reduced him to an estate with a pool and a four-car garage. Students, ever the realists, protested that the inclusion of the pool was not justifiable. The same issue of *Landscape Architecture* heralded the appointment of Earle Draper as head of the Division of Land Planning and Housing for the Tennessee Valley Authority. The past and present were on a collision course.

The agenda for the thirty-fifth annual meeting of the American Society of Landscape Architects, held in January, 1934, underscores this confluence of past and present. The principal speakers were Arthur E. Morgan, the controversial chairman of the Board of Directors of the TVA, and Arno Cammerer, National Parks director. But the evening entertainment consisted of a conversation on the topic of "What Makes a Fine Art of Landscape Architecture" and a film on Italian gardens. Although tantalized by the potential of the public landscape, for purposes of relaxation the landscape architect still turned to the quotidian Italian garden.

A new generation of designers commanded the scene, a generation raised on Platt's *Italian Gardens* and Edith Wharton's *Italian Villas and their Gardens*, not on Capability Brown or Humphrey Repton and the English landscape school. This flood tide of landscape architects—Michael Rapuano,

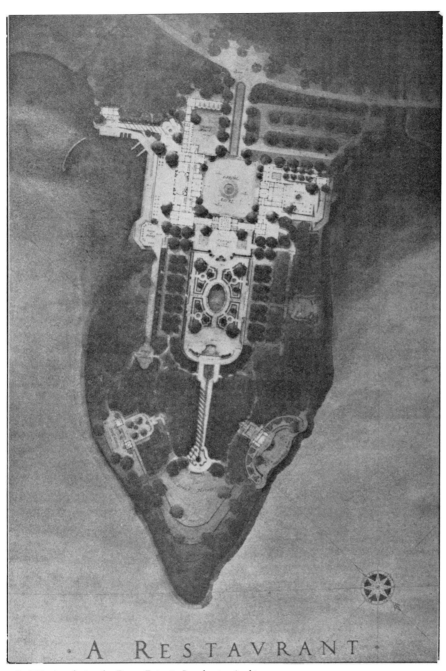

A RESTAVRANT

26. *Winning design for Rome Prize in Landscape Architecture, 1933.*

27. *Conservatory Garden, Central Park, aerial view, 1935.*

Gilmore Clarke, Norman Newton, Prentiss French, and A. D. Taylor among others—introduced rose gardens, garden theaters, and parterres to the lilting meadows and cursive woods of the English pleasure ground. Beaux Arts gardens settled in alongside the invasive play lots, tennis courts, and ball fields. At the same time that twenty marginal playgrounds infiltrated the hallowed pastoral precincts of Central Park, a full formal garden complex materialized in the northeast corner below The Mount and next to Harlem Meer. Typical of New York's extreme response, the Conservatory Garden offers no less than three of the stock Beaux Arts garden types (fig. 27). In the center is the arbor or mall garden, and flanking it are a rose garden and box or evergreen garden. An intricate wrought-iron arbor hung with wisteria crowns a bank at the head of the green swath (fig. 28). In the flagstone floor of the arbor are set medallions representing the thirteen original colonies. Flagstone paths gird the *tapis vert* and join before the arbor around a fountain pool (fig. 29).

Shorn of iron tracery, flagstone, and bas reliefs, the basic format of a mall garden—turfed with perimeter paths and fronted by a pool and arbor—made its debut in this country in 1901 in Charles Platt's seminal, but no longer extant Garden of Weld in Brookline, Massachusetts (fig. 30). This garden was featured, along with his other work, in Platt's extremely influential 1913 monograph, which went through three editions in the space of a dozen years.[4] Platt doubtless observed numerous mall gardens in his travels in Italy. Usually a structure more imposing than an arbor anchored the garden, such as the tall, semicircular four-part gateway which terminates the long panel at the right

28. *Conservatory Garden, Central Park, arbor.*

29. *Conservatory Garden, Central Park, arbor garden.*

end of the Villa Farnese at Caprarola (fig. 31). By necessity, American translations generally reduced the grandeur of their European sources. In the Garden
of Weld and its Depression-era imitations, such as the garden of the Little
Theater in Raleigh, North Carolina or the mall variation in Lakecliffe Park in
Dallas, the arbor is a simple structure of stone and wood or wood post and beam
(figs. 32, 33).

The Dallas garden skews the arbor and takes other liberties with the
classic composition, but by far the most radical transformation of the mall
garden is the National Mall in the nation's capitol. Three eminent landscape
architects—Ferrucio Vitale, Gilmore Clarke, and Henry Hubbard—executed
the McMillan Commission plans drawn up in 1902 by Daniel Burnham,
Charles McKim, and Frederick Law Olmsted, Jr. Instead of a small pool and a
pergola, an expansive reflecting pool and the gargantuan Capitol Building
confront the long grass rectangle crisscrossed by walks and bounded by Inde-
pendence and Constitution Avenues. In this exceptional instance the expansion rather than reduction of a European precedent produced a classic American form. When in 1936 the Public Works Administration installed this blend
of European garden and urban practice, the vacant position for spatial symbol
of American nationalistic pride was at last filled.

With somewhat less dramatic results, Americans also adopted the cascade from the lexicon of the Renaissance garden. The Italians delighted in the
play of water; many a villa deployed a water source to create a rill descending a
set of stairs footed by a pool or basin. The Villa Farnese's greatest triumph is

30. *Garden of Weld, Brookline, Massachusetts, plan.*

31. *Villa Farnese, Caprarola, plan.*

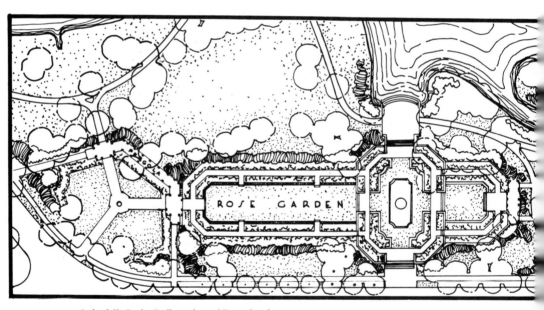

32. *Lakecliffe Park, Dallas, plan of Rose Garden.*

33. *Little Theater Rose Garden, Raleigh, North Carolina.*

not the panel and its flanking tripartite gardens but the splendid water cascade on the opposite side (fig. 34). In the United States, the Meridian Hill Cascade four blocks north of the White House was the first among numerous public water ramps to be built (fig. 35). Adorned with planting designed by the eminent firm of Vitale and Geiffert, the cascade formally opened in 1932. The spreading upper terrace, the loggia, the parallel sets of steps, the prominent walls and decorative urns and balusters have their source in the Villa Farnese cascade at Caprarola. Indeed, Meridian Hill matches its Italian source more closely than any subsequent American cascade, but differences are apparent. The scale is smaller, and the Washington ramp incorporates planting directly within the architectural program. American informality allowed a glade of trees instead of a parterre and substitution of concrete for stone. The changes all represent reduction dictated by taste, budget, climate, and, perhaps most important, difference in function. Arbor and cascade here serve as backdrops for incidental relaxation, not as stages for Renaissance ritual and pomp. But its designers could not have divined exactly how casual use of the cascade would become. Vitale and Geiffert never guessed that the Meridian Hill Cascade would one day be frequented by inner-city ghetto children. Many of the formal spaces created during the Depression have proven adaptable to a variety of fates and, indeed, have often survived better than modern parks especially tailored to specific socioeconomic or ethnic groups.

In their scheme for the water ramp at Trinity Park in Fort Worth in

34. *Villa Farnese Cascade, Caprarola.*

35. *Meridian Hill Park Cascade, Washington, D.C.*

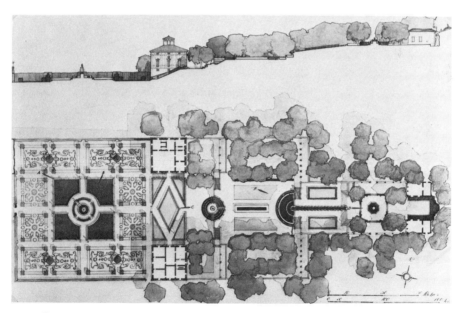

36. *Villa Lante, Bagnaia, plan.*

1934, the firm of Hare and Hare was avowedly imitating the Villa Lante of Bagnaia in the vicinity of Florence (figs. 36, 37), but they did even more rearranging than did the architects of Meridian Hill. Beginning at the top, they substituted an open-sided shelter for the twin loges. They condensed a series of sculptural fountains into a single water spout set in an arch of the shelter's terrace wall. The water chain passes not through a passageway of boxwood and olives, but through three diamond-shaped planting beds lined with yaupon and roses. A simple pond rather than an elaborate, architectonic basin completes the program. The Fort Worth cascade exhibits even further the tendency for American translations to diminish the architectural program while enhancing the horticultural dimension.

This tendency became even more pronounced when the city of Oakland, California offered, also in 1934, its version of the Villa Lante tradition.[5] Balcony, balustrade, shelters, and any pretense of a loggia have vanished (fig. 38). Even the stairs which accompanied the other cascades have been leveled into paved paths. The roses that in Texas tamely escorted the water down its course have here escaped their beds and sweep up the sides of the bowl-shaped site at the base of the Oakland hills. The floral spectacle has here become ascendent, elbowing the cascade to an ancillary position off to the side of the main axis of the garden. Clearly the landscape architect has taken distinct horticultural and compositional license.

37. *Trinity Park Rose Garden, Fort Worth, perspective.*

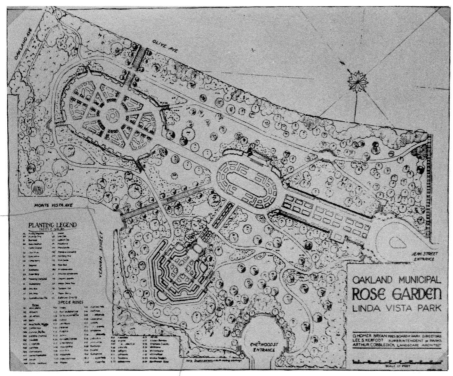

38. *Oakland Municipal Rose Garden, plan.*

Free-wheeling American adaptations did not always work. The designer of a mongrel Italianate garden in Antelope Park in Lincoln, Nebraska proceeded too timidly. A dais all of four feet tall overviews a green swath lined with a ragged bed of roses and bisected by a concrete path leading to two innocuous fountains (fig. 39). This jumble of elements does not even begin to recreate an Old World ambience on the back of the Great Plains.

A jumble of traditions that exudes both Old World elegance and New World adventure, the Berkeley Municipal Rose Garden embodies eclectic finesse (fig. 40). The Berkeley garden masterfully blends the three chief Italianate motifs—the arbor, the cascade, and the theater—and then douses them with roses, the favorite floral symbol of the thirties. Wreathed by a wooden arbor, a series of terraces abloom with color step down the steep slope to form a bowl-shaped auditorium, where appears a gushing rivulet at the bottom midpoint. The Berkeley garden, which the WPA worked on from 1933 to 1937, symbolizes the American relaxation of continental practice.

A second cascade in Oakland, constructed in 1936, exemplifies even more cogently than the Berkeley garden the burgeoning of a native landscape style (fig. 41). The overall format of the water course unmistakeably derives from the precedents of the Villas Lante and Caprarola. The water flows from

39. *Antelope Park Rose Garden, Lincoln, Nebraska.*

40. *Berkeley Municipal Rose Garden, Berkeley, California.*

41. Woodminster Cascade, 1984, *Oakland, California*
   (Original ink drawing by Judith Clancy, © 1984).

the back of a theater designed to simulate a loggia; it then descends on a direct axial line to two basins on separate levels. A formal staircase lined with olive trees connects the two pools; symmetrical planting beds adjoin the central axis. Despite the conventional formality of the balanced, terraced composition, the cascade itself diverges from its models. A scenario intended to approximate indigenous wilderness has replaced the controlled architectural program. Ponderous slabs and picturesque boulders have preempted the sequence of scalloped basins and steps that formerly composed the chain. Lofty redwoods and scarlet pyracantha cluster in place of clipped boxwood. So determined were the designers to emulate nature that they imported the slabs for the cascade from the distant Sierras. The Woodminster Cascade both carries on and liberates the tradition of the Italian water chain.

The Woodminster Cascade incorporated a naturalism that was more prevalent in the domain of large-scale planning and design, specifically of state, national, and regional parks. A proclivity for native materials and plants and free-flowing landscape forms also occurs in the rebellious Midwest heartland dominated by Frank Lloyd Wright and landscape designer Jens Jensen, who was active into the thirties. In Milwaukee's Boerner Botanical Garden or Chicago's Lincoln Park visitors can explore leafy bowers with secluded lily ponds (figs. 16, 42). Burrowing deeper into the Midwest, tourists could unearth a fantastic tableau worthy of Alice in Wonderland in the old fort town of Kearney, Nebraska. Rocky channels delineate a rivulet which winds over miniature cliffs to spill at last into a frog pool, over which a whimsical, dovecote-like stone tower presides (figs. 43, 44). The picturesque treatment of water diverges altogether from the demonstrations in clarity and logic posed by the Washington, Fort Worth, and Berkeley heirs to the Italian Renaissance, but all these gardens share the love for the exotic which characterizes so much of the Depression work.

Despite its digression into sylvan reveries, Kearney's Harmon Park could stand as a model for thirties park planning. Its few acres strike an ideal balance of active and passive recreation forms: a large pool and bathhouse, tennis courts, and an outdoor amphitheater. A rock garden substitutes for an organized ornamental garden area; nevertheless, the conjunction of garden and sport is typical of the time.

A wide variety of planting represents another trait of accomplished thirties park design. The American renditions of Renaissance formats already showed a tendency for the floral element to assert itself. In the Berkeley or Oakland gardens a single species takes over, but in Gilmore Clarke's 1936 plan for Colonial Park in Harlem a great range of plants clothe the park's rocky

42. Lincoln Park, Chicago, rock garden.

43. Harmon Park, Kearney, Nebraska, rock garden.

slopes. A contemporary plan for the site might call for three or four different deciduous trees and at most five or six kinds of shrubs, but Clarke specifies seven varieties of deciduous trees, two kinds of evergreen trees, and fourteen species of shrubs. In comparison, the plant list for a "naturalistic garden theater" for a private residence in Brookline, Massachusetts circa 1924 enumerated 20 types of deciduous trees, 21 species of evergreen, 52 kinds of shrubs, and 110 different perennials.[6] Although munificent by contemporary standards, Clarke's Depression park was actually a simplification of the country estate, just as the country estate pared down the architectural effusiveness of its Italian sources.

Distilled, numerous traditions went into the parks of the thirties. En-

44. *Harmon Park, Kearney, Nebraska, tower.*

glish parks, public and private, and the American country estate, with its prototypical combination of sport and garden, contributed heavily. Transmitted both through the estate tradition and independently of it, the Italian example was paramount and peculiar to this decade. Frank Waugh boasted that, if American garden art did not outdo the "noble models of the Italian Renaissance" in quality, they may well have matched in quantity. The volume of New Deal production facilitated the rise of an indigenous style that in the fifties established American landscape design as a paradigm for Europe and beyond.

CHAPTER FOUR

The Recreation Migration: Metropolitan Parks and Parkways

ROSE GARDENS AND WATER CHAINS afforded Depression America escape with sophistication, but these continental accretions did not satisfy a populace that had only recently come in from the barn and the woodlot. In the 1920s the U.S. for the first time became a predominately urban nation, with over half of its population in urban areas. For such a newly urbanized citizenry, no garden and, for that matter, no baseball diamond could substitute for forest and field.[1]

Cities, promoting their own growth and the growth of mobility, sought to expand their recreational holdings beyond play lots and pleasure grounds. In response to the people's restless, nostalgic yearnings for the woods, politicians converted outlying tracts into park land. Furthermore, park authorities acknowledged the importance of the car by creating the parkway. Ideally, the parkway was meant as a transitional "green" zone in the intensifying search for the bucolic. But the parks and preserves, like the acquisition of treasure, sparked desire for more remote and purer enclaves of nature. By the time the metropolitan park concept reached the West Coast, planners condemned the use of automobiles within the preserves and shunned the parkway.

The urge for unspoiled country spanned a wide cross-section of the population. At the top, Roosevelt, in his first term in office, tried to secure an official mountain retreat in nearby Maryland. Near the bottom, young men were signing up in droves for the Civilian Conservation Corps in order to test their strength against the wilds. In their turn, local government officials employed CCC brawn to consolidate their rural preserves, so in this area of recreation expansion sentiment and reality conjoined. The forces existed to fulfill the need. As part of this need, the metropolitan park became the first in a migration that encompassed, further afield, state and national parks.

Neither metropolitan parks nor the parkway was new to the landscape. Boston had introduced a nexus of metropolitan parks and a rudimentary form of the parkway as early as the 1870s. Midwestern cities such as Cleveland, Chicago, and Milwaukee had started reserving ambient countryside between 1914 and 1920. The rural areas thus acquired were largely neglected until the creation of the CCC in 1933 offered a fortuitous, gratuitous work force. With the advent of the CCC and other New Deal resources, existing ex-urban arteries began to pulsate and new ones took shape. During the Depression decade, the terms *metropolitan, county,* and *regional* were commonly used to define land preserves created for recreational purposes outside city limits. In general, larger cities such as Cleveland formed *metropolitan parks,* while smaller cities such as Phoenix founded *county parks.* Whichever designation was adopted, between 1925 and 1935 these park expanses more than doubled in acreage.[2]

After witnessing the development of prototypical parkways in the Boston area, New York borrowed the idea and began, in 1907, the Bronx River Parkway, the landscaped road that first defined the term. Strictly interpreted, the term *parkway* applies to a self-contained and uninterrupted stretch of road, landscaped and appointed with recreational facilities. Inspired by the success of the Bronx River Parkway, in 1922 Westchester County organized a county-wide network of parks and parkways that became a model for large-scale recreation work in the thirties. But New York, at first a champion of the parkway, later became its nemesis.

During the Depression, road construction of all kinds became a high priority. Because this basic occupation could absorb large numbers of the unskilled and unemployed, Washington helped fund construction even of minor arteries. Although the thirties road campaign consisted mainly of the WPA rolling out farm-to-market roads, the general surge in road construction assured the increasing dependence of recreation upon the automobile. The parkway, which made up a tiny but visible portion of federal spending, was the most obvious manifestation of this phenomenon.

The parkway, if it was to fulfill its role as a strip of land primarily dedicated to recreation and secondarily to transportation, had to offer amenities like ample landscaping and clearances for vistas and picnic shelters. Since no unauthorized obstacle, whether bridge, road, or building, was to intrude upon the air or land rights, the end result was a strip of visual pleasure insulated from commercial or business pursuits.

So described, the parkway would seem the antithesis of the needs of New York City, which in 1930 boasted but two unfinished through routes. Not one uninterrupted road bypassed the maze of Brooklyn's streets in the direction of Long Island, and crowded onto this antiquated road network was an automobile population that had increased over sixfold in the years 1920 to 1935. However, parkways predated freeways, and relief labor was restricted to "park access roads" and landscaped routes.[3] Robert Moses, czar of the Long Island

State Park Commission, the State Parks Council, the New York City Parks Commission, and the Triborough Bridge Authority, was determined to build roads in whatever form he could most easily get them.

In order to accommodate Demon Traffic, Moses deformed the concept of the parkway to suit New York's purposes. For the main artery affording access to the west side of Manhattan, he wedged six lanes of highway between the Hudson River and the remodeled Riverside Park far above. Six lanes of metal and rubber overwhelms almost all appreciation for the nearby river and vegetation.

At least the Henry Hudson Parkway has not expanded; many of the New York "parkways" of the 1930s have been enlarged, destroying any tenuous links with nature that might have originally existed. No one in his or her right mind would consider a picnic alongside the Grand Central Parkway that connects Manhattan with Long Island and LaGuardia Airport. Roads like the Henry Hudson Parkway, the Grand Central Parkway, the Cross-Island, the Gowanus, and the Interborough, all installed in the New York area during the Depression, made a mockery of the original vision of a parkway as a strip of land containing a road. Yet by 1940 New York could claim more miles of uninterrupted highway than the nation's next five largest cities combined.[4] To his credit, Moses was able to wheedle seventy-five miles of "parkway" and three bridges out of Washington, while Chicago could only manage to streamline its one principal artery, Lakeshore Drive.

Critics, led by Robert Caro in his biography, *The Power Broker: Robert Moses and the Fall of New York*, have lambasted the city's former park and parkway impresario for the frenzy of road development which peaked with the so-called parkways of the thirties. In his hefty polemic, Caro blames Moses for the disintegration through neglect of public transportation and for the obliteration of the waterfront and previously unspoiled natural oases. But, in defense of Moses, New York instigated changes which were also being sought in smaller cities where the glamor of the automobile was likewise commanding political obeisance. In New York the Astoria Ferry bowed before the mighty Triborough; on the West Coast the passenger-only ferry system crumbled before the San Francisco–Oakland Bay Bridge, completed in 1936. What distinguished New York City's parkway program and bridge construction was the intensity with which they were pursued. The parkways were not, for the most part, parkways at all, but then the notion of a freeway was just germinating. New York made an original contribution to road development early in the decade with the completion of the Bronx River Parkway and then set the pace again, creating a singularly advanced system to aid uninterrupted traffic flow. In essence, New York City solved its transportation dilemma through the same replication that produced the multiple playgrounds and parks.

While the need to design for volume caused New York to diverge from the strict definition of a parkway, it was conforming with other cities in its coupling of highways with rivers. Manhattan's achievement during this decade in asphalting its two shorelines was no aberration. Everywhere roads were monopolizing riverbanks. In the Midwest, Milwaukee adorned a number of its streams with parkways, hoping to boost land values.[5] With CCC assistance, New Jersey and Pennsylvania developed the interconnected Cooper River and Egg Harbor River Parkways. The CCC also labored to build New Jersey's Rahway River Parkway and the extension of the Hutchinson River Parkway north of New York City. The District of Columbia paneled the Potomac with the George Washington Memorial Parkway. New England considered plans for one road to run the length of the Merrimack and skim the tops of the Green and White Mountain ranges. But World War II intervened in plans to build the most extravagent river road of all. During the war, the proposed National Mississippi River Parkway disappeared into the labyrinth of Congress, appearing only years later in diluted form when the mania for parkways had subsided.

Practical and aesthetic reasoning inspired this predilection for riverside parkways. Roads, not rivers, were the routes of leisure in the twenties and thirties. The National Resources Board claimed that recreation accounted for 60 percent of road use in the United States in 1933.[6] Rivers were ignored, considered little more than dumps by park officials, who saw parkways as their salvation. (The Bronx River Parkway originated as a project to clean up the decayed Bronx River.) In their eyes, rivers did not merit contact or even close contemplation. With the exception of two limited areas—one of eight blocks and another of two—the 6.7 mile Henry Hudson Parkway restricts use of the Hudson's east bank along Manhattan to passing motorists (fig. 45). Excluding this ten-block reprieve, the bank of the Hudson from 72d to 125th Street consists of an almost inaccessible narrow strip of weeds penetrated here and there by dirt paths. From 125th Street past 200th the parkway is elevated, the park tapers into obscurity, and the bank of the river remains remote and neglected. At the park's epicenter in the West 80s and 90s, pedestrians stroll along a grand concourse and gaze out over ball fields and the so-called parkway onto the Hudson (fig. 46). When questioned about the alienation of the pedestrian from the river, Gilmore Clarke, landscape architect for the rehabilitation of Riverside Park and design consultant for the parkway, responded that the Hudson "is, and will be for some time, an open sewer; hence pedestrian access to it was thought to be undesirable."[7] Rivers were thus reduced to backdrops to be scanned at modern speeds.

Business and commuter travel did not overwhelm all ten of New York's Depression-era parkways. The exclusion of commercial vehicles preserves the character of verdant stretches of the Southern State or Belt Parkways. To follow the narrow lanes and bosques of the Bronx River Parkway, which suddenly give way to the melée of modern Manhattan, is to experience a present-day parallel of Rip Van Winkle's awakening. For their first few months New York City's parkways may truly have made available, as Moses proclaimed

45. *Henry Hudson Parkway, New York.*

they would, the "benefits of light and air."[8] The problem of carbon monoxide emissions was not apparent to the early planners and backers.

The CCC-sponsored parkway systems of Milwaukee and Cleveland offer a consoling contrast. Substantially upholstered by verdure, they retain their bucolic intent. An impression of remoteness and tranquility—the pastoral city park attenuated for the convenience of the automobile—still charac-terizes these Midwestern parkways (fig. 47). Milwaukee's Root River, Honey

46. Riverside Park Mall, New York.

Creek, and Oak Creek Parkways decorously complement streams, while firmly adhering to the function of providing access to parks. Similarly, in the Cleveland area, the Strongsville–Brecksville River Parkway exists principally to connect the Strongsville and Brecksville Reservations. Urbanization has not eroded the recreational character of these roads; the recreational purport of New York's parkway system was suspect from the start.

The parkways of Milwaukee, Cleveland, and even New York pale before the Blue Ridge, the consummate parkway of the thirties. The Blue Ridge is to the parkway what the Appalachian Trail—another product of the Depression era—is to the footpath. Four hundred and eighty-four miles in length, the Blue Ridge connects Shenandoah National Park in Virginia with the Great Smoky National Park in Tennessee. One of the largest of the Roosevelt Administration's projects, the Blue Ridge epitomizes New Deal perceptions and methods. In fact, its funding was part of the first major act of Roosevelt's presidency. All the prominent New Deal agencies shared in its construction, which began in 1936. Virginia and North Carolina provided the rights of way, the PWA bankrolled it, the National Park Service and the Bureau of Public Roads choreographed it, and the CCC and the WPA prepared the land and built the recreational facilities. Each agency had a role and all cooperated in a manner characteristic of other larger-scale operations. For instance, if the CCC exceeded its $1,500-per-unit ceiling cost, the PWA made up the difference. Yet another New Deal amalgam, the Resettlement Administration,

47. Rocky River Parkway, Cleveland.

helped by securing the land for a system of wayside parks distributed at thirty-mile intervals, with larger parks for overnight stays at sixty-mile intervals.

One NPS landscape architect who worked for ten years on this monumental road recalls the setting upon which this high-powered collusion of New Deal forces descended:

The area of the BRP [Blue Ridge Parkway] was very primitive in 1936: oxen still on the plows, cows hitched to carts, only dirt roads, little stores that dealt with due bills instead of money, houses heated by fireplaces—only many even without an outhouse. One valley with intermarrying and dimwitted people. Next valley good morals and intelligent people. One section the natives spoke pure Elizabethan English and a group came over from England to study them.[9]

Here on a mountain range was the lost America, quintessential dream of the New Deal. Viewed from a parkway at thirty-five miles per hour, this could pass as Jeffersonian, agrarian democracy in action.

The New Deal apotheosis of this backward bit of America betrays the intensity of the romantic consciousness of the Depression period. The Scenic, as the Parkway was known to the locals, was intended to have minimum impact upon the territory it traversed, other than enhancing its cultural legacy and natural beauty. The road itself is minimal—two lanes, thirty feet wide, and curvilinear—aspects that enforce its maximum speed limit of forty miles per hour. Still today the style and pacing of the road orient the traveler to the measured rhythm of mountain life. The frequent waysides beckon like a call from the porch to "come set a while." The fields of crops and pastureland set the scene and no clues betray that they have been painstakingly preserved. Like props in a play, post-and-rail fencing, a grist mill, and a storied midwife's cabin enhance the aura of nostalgia. More than an excursion into rural and mountain scenery, the Blue Ridge Parkway conjures up an agrarian and wilderness past.

Periods of stress have fomented nostalgic yearnings before and since the Great Depression. Vincent Scully traces the Colonial Revival and the Shingle Style of the 1870s to a reaction against the corruption, hardship, and growing materialism of those flaccid times. The Depression also prompted longings for the past. In 1929 came the collapse of the stock market and the beginning of the restoration of colonial Williamsburg. During this period three parkway projects strove to connect the nation with its eighteenth-century past. The first of these, the Natchez Trace, runs between Natchez, Mississippi and Natchez, Tennessee. Originally an old Indian trail, it once served as the homeward route for Kentucky boatmen who floated lumber rafts to New Orleans. Work began on the Colonial Parkway in 1923 and continued through the 1930s. The Colonial Parkway linked Yorktown with the old capitol of Williamsburg. The Mt. Vernon Memorial Parkway, the first federally built parkway to cast off from Washington, wound into rural Virginia to George Washington's historic home. Like the pilgrimage roads of Medieval Europe, these highways signified a quest for ideals and for a lost and ennobled past.

In its pursuit of beautiful scenery and an idealized past the parkways fashion broached megalomania. The Blue Ridge Parkway was intended to be only a brief section of a pan-Appalachian way which was to extend from the Canadian border to Georgia. The nation's foremost town planner, John Nolen, helped create the preliminary plan for the section which traversed the Green Mountains. If it had been built, the road would have prohibited all future opportunity for skiing at Killington, Bromley, Mt. Mansfield and Jay Peak. In the fever of the moment, the journal *American Forests*, not usually a haven for radicalism, visualized "a master highway system which will link all National Parks, Monuments, and historical sites."[10] Such extreme expressions of the automotive adventuring spirit finally began to stir some opposition. The same year *American Forests* published its utopian vision, Robert Marshall, Forest Service official and founder of the Wilderness Society, condemned road-building through primeval forests at the annual meeting of the American Forestry Association, singling out for special attack the "popular ridge roads."[11] But despite the grandiose plans and Marshall's fears, the parkway-related scenic roads did not in the end constitute a major invasionary force of the country's wilderness.

Although protectionists disapproved of automotive encroachment upon the historic wilds, pedestrian forays into the back country received support from all sides. The New Deal investment in conservation made possible the completion of the two most ambitious wilderness trails in the nation—the parallel but widely separated Appalachian and Pacific Crest Trails. Both originated during the years between the World Wars. Forester-philosopher Benton MacKaye dreamed up the Appalachian Trail in 1921. The idea was revived in 1926 and by the grace of the CCC realized in 1937. A year later the federal government declared protected a two-mile-wide trail zone along the length of the footpath.[12] Private wilderness groups worked on the Pacific Crest Trail in the 1930s. As of 1935 the CCC had transformed it into a passable trail threading 2,265 miles through the Sierras—200 miles longer than the Appalachian Trail. Through the making of these trails the era's love of the pioneer past attained transcontinental proportions.

The parkways never attained transcontinental proportions, but proliferated along with metropolitan, county, and regional parks while the traditional urban pastoral park declined. The concept of the inner-city pastoral retreat was losing favor. A host of sports and game facilities invaded Central Park and Golden Gate Park, while, according to a 1935 National Park Service survey, cities increasingly dedicated new public acreage to swimming pools, beaches, golf courses, and athletic fields.[13] The better-qualified ex-urban park now served as a rural refuge.

As with the parkways, the Midwest played a dominant role in the development of the ex-urban land preserve. The Civilian Conservation Corps transformed a series of scattered holdings around Chicago into a public recreation resource connected by a network of trails, roads, picnic areas, and parking lots. One extensive area, neighboring the home territory of Secretary of the Interior Harold Ickes, boasted the largest concentration of CCC camps in the nation. Twenty camps in the vicinity of Skokie transformed an extensive swamp into a shaded expanse of picnic lawns, rambling roads, and graceful lagoons. Cleveland, which by 1935 enjoyed, after Chicago, the nation's second highest concentration of park land per capita, also benefitted from the good timing of the CCC. Even into the 1970s, an estimated 75 percent of Cleveland parkland—including 15 footbridges, 30 acres of picnic ground, 72 acres of sites for vista viewing, 9 lakes, and 46 miles of foot trails—was the handiwork of FDR's "Tree Army."[14] Encouraged by Cleveland's example, in 1931 four other Ohio cities established similar metropolitan park systems that likewise profited from the labor pool of the New Deal. In this way the Midwest was provided with ample opportunity to build upon the earlier city planning experiments of the East Coast.

The ex-urban park ultimately extended to the Pacific coast as well. In the Southwest, Phoenix had, prior to 1933, gathered fifteen thousand acres of desert land into its South Mountain Park—a land grab surpassed in size only by those of Chicago, Boston, and Westchester. In Phoenix, the CCC occupied itself with ten picnic ramadas, employee housing, a concessionary, and a stable, among other projects. In the Rockies, Denver seconded Phoenix's metropolitan park empire with its chain of mountain parks, one of which contains the spectacular CCC-constructed Red Rocks Amphitheater (fig. 48). In 1934 on the California coast, the seven cities lining the Berkeley–Oakland Hills approved the creation of a vast regional park which preserved a sizeable portion of the surrounding hills for recreation. The East Bay Park District officially acquired the land for the first three parks in 1936.

Their subsequent pattern of development involved the increasing dominance of the National Park Service, which more and more governed the development of parkways and metropolitan parks, especially in the West and South, which had little prior history of recreation and conservation activity. The emergence of the National Park Service both conformed with and encouraged a proclivity for greater naturalism in large-scale park settings. Toward the end of the decade, the nation lost its fear of the phenomenon of leisure and began to accept it as a given. Correspondingly, the landscape settings relaxed. In Oakland, rose gardens and regional parks alike flexed their design elements more freely. The National Park Service coached the maturing regional park.

Even before official approval was gained for the parks, WPA laborers and CCC enrollees were busy digging up Tilden Park, the foremost of the

48. Red Rocks Park Amphitheater, Denver.

original four parks of the East Bay complex. By 1937 the WPA had plowed a road through this hilly expanse of eucalyptus-dotted grassland in order to install a golf course. The golf course, a favorite with both the public and the park administrators because it provided profit as well as recreation, was the forward wedge of a whole squadron of athletic pursuits—football, baseball, track, basketball, handball, and volleyball—incorporated into a master plan of about 1935. The plan also detailed a boulevard complete with rondpoint bordering the park and a grid pattern of roads extending out from the athletic area (fig. 49). Though only a preliminary study and eventually rejected, this plan cast Tilden in the sporting mode of thirties parks.

But in 1939 the East Bay Regional Park District reevaluated development in Tilden and adopted an alternative plan, sponsored by the NPS, that confirmed the national trend toward more naturalistic treatment of metropolitan park areas (fig. 50). The new plan confined alterations to the area south of the road, where the WPA had already built the golf course. On the north side, the revised NPS scheme limited improvements to trails, picnic areas, minimal roads, and the inevitable lake.

Tilden, nevertheless, still descends in a direct line from the pastoral image perfected by Capability Brown and Humphrey Repton in eighteenth-century England. Before it was a park, Spanish-owned sheep following on the heels of loggers formed the grassy hillsides. In 1940 the East Bay Regional Park District veered from this essentially agricultural pattern and built one of the first wilderness areas to be part of an ex-urban park system. The NPS plan for Redwood Regional Park preserved almost intact a magnificent redwood-clad stretch of slopes and valley. Only the obligatory fire road and a few trails intrude upon this pristine forest. The plan restricts roads, play areas, and picnic sites to the periphery. The forested reaches of this preserve, so different

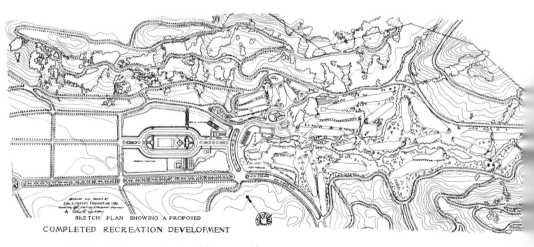

49. *Tilden Park, Berkeley, rejected master plan, ca. 1935.*

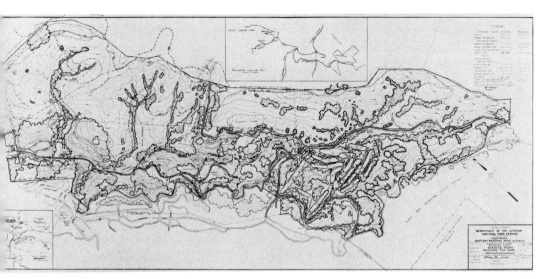

50. *Tilden Park, Berkeley, accepted master plan, 1938.*

from the grazed slopes of Tilden, acclaim the primacy of the National Park
Service's influence in late New Deal park design.

In the first few years of the New Deal, the National Park Service would
not have been capable of a Redwood Regional Park. Although from the start
the NPS cooperated with local and state authorities on technical and design
matters, the rapid generation of parks at all levels strained its limited design
resources. At the inception of the Emergency Conservation Work program,
the NPS design staff consisted of ten landscape architects, five building architects, and one structural engineer. This small crew was based in San Francisco
with one regional office in Washington. By 1935 the number of professionals
in the Branch of Plans and Designs had jumped to 120. Then came the Park,
Parkway and Recreational Study Act of 1936, which officially sanctioned
federal involvement in metropolitan and state park planning, a move that
enabled the National Park Service's name to appear on local plans such as the
master plan for Tilden Park. The year this act passed the NPS staff in San
Francisco almost doubled in size.

The following year witnessed yet another critical step in the expansion
of the Park Service. In 1937, a significant year for many of the New Deal
agencies, the Park Service regionalized. The Park Service had from the beginning recognized that decentralization was necessary in order to meet the
challenge of the national public works bonanza. Because state, regional, and
metropolitan park work comprised a large portion of the supervisory responsibilities of the federal park agency, the Service established a number of district
offices. The effectiveness of the regional operation convinced the NPS to
entrust to the various districts the management of CCC work in national parks

as well. Finally, in 1937, the entire NPS apparatus was revamped on a regional basis, a system that persists to the present. The regionalization of the National Park Service was inevitable as the territory and responsibilities of the national parks increased, but the ferment of the thirties helped precipitate the change.

Aside from generating and shaping bureaucracies, the spate of federal money allocated to recreation and conservation allowed the New Deal to revive old plans and support ongoing lines of design talent. The New Deal completed some of the neglected projects of Frederick Law Olmsted, including Aquatic Park in San Francisco and Cleveland's Metropolitan Park District. The National Mall, which stretches from the Washington Monument to the Capitol Building, utilized the ideas and talent of five generations of planners, from Pierre Charles L'Enfant, the engineer who, in the eighteenth century, originally laid out the Mall, to Frederick Olmsted, Jr. in the twentieth. In 1930, the firm Olmsted Brothers, begun by Olmsted, Sr. and carried on by his son, prepared the master plan which specified the areas of the Berkeley–Oakland hills to be reserved for a regional park. Under Frederick Law Olmsted, Jr., the firm also prepared California's influential 1928 State Park Plan. Hence, through the revival of old projects and a continuity of professional expertise, thirties landscaping ventures capitalized upon ideas that originated as early as 1790.

Heirs to landscape talents and practices other than that of Olmsted profited from the new-found government patronage. Conrad Wirth, executive supervisor of CCC work for the National Park Service, had grown up in Hartford and Minneapolis where his father, Theodore, had helped plan and build those cities' parks. Prentiss French, nephew of the sculptor Daniel Chester French, and son of C. E. French, who was a partner of the influential landscape architect Horace Cleveland in Chicago, supervised CCC crews in Florida during two winters. His tales of the Civilian Conservation Corps indicate that the demands of the recreation movement taxed all the skills of the landscape architects of the day.

Prepared by an education at Harvard, travel in Europe, and work with Olmsted Brothers, Prentiss French tackled two metropolitan parks, the first winter with a crew of brazen youths from the Hell's Kitchen section of New York, and the next with a gang of country boys from deep in the heart of Georgia. During the first winter French was forced to court-martial eight of his laborers. Yet he and his band of street toughs still managed to produce a huge entrance made of hatchet-cut stone, a stone bridge, and a hill that became the highest point in Dade County. Assigned the next winter to build Tampa's Hillsborough River County Park with the more skilled and compliant Georgians, French found his problem to be not so much discipline as the absence of construction materials. For the park shelter he set his men to fashioning shakes out of the local tidewater red cypress and hewing posts from palm trees. He scrounged material for the floor from the streets of an abandoned subdivision bankrupted by the Depression. Although it is probably now defunct—as French points out, palm trees do not make lasting columns—this shelter symbolized the design-by-wit that emerged from the chemistry of hard times, mental agility, and professional self-esteem.[15]

The ex-urban park and parkway served as much-needed rural escapes from the city. They were considered a vital part of public recreation, and a large amount of Depression labor was devoted to their development. During this period, respect for unadulterated natural settings grew, as seen in comparing the forested slopes of Redwood Regional Park with the large-scale parks built earlier in the decade. Milwaukee's Whitnall Park, for example, was a rural expanse, but one refined by an elegant botanical garden, a rambling parkway, and a golf course, in the style also adopted in Tilden Park. Tilden stands as a halfway point between the horticultural and sports-minded older park and the naturalistic new breed best represented by Redwood.

With the large-scale parkway and ex-urban park the liberalizing tendencies seen already at work in formal garden design now become paramount. The Blue Ridge Parkway, the Denver Metropolitan Parks, and the East Bay Regional Park system proclaim the indigenous landscape. The National Park Service, which by definition espoused the native environment, took command. State and national parks transcend the once-dominant European design. Like the WPA guide books, theater, and murals, metropolitan parks and parkways celebrate the American scene, stressing a heroic past. Like the plays, the literature, and the painting, Depression-era landscape reveals the nation to itself.

CHAPTER FIVE

Resorting to the Woods: State Parks and Recreation Demonstration Areas

EVEN MORE THAN PARKWAYS, playgrounds, and metropolitan parks, state parks were a product of the Depression. During the New Deal these recreation landscapes developed to a level of crude finish and beauty unequaled before or since. The Recreation Demonstration Areas, which were a kind of training ground for the state park, began, flourished, and died with the New Deal.

The sober, orderly playground conveys a sense of the crusading moralism of the Depression era, while, in contrast, the lush rose garden and lyrical cascade suggest a strong vein of romanticism. The parkway and the metropolitan park underscore the period's historic pride and growing national self-awareness. The state park and the Recreation Demonstration Area embody all these qualities and more. In particular, the state park of the thirties expresses the cherished New Deal ideals of coexistence with nature, even if man-made, and communal living, in the pure sense of shared labor and play. From Oregon to Tennessee the harmonious settings formed by these high-minded ideals have survived more intact than almost any other genre of Depression landscape. Visitors to the placid woods, lakes, and cabin clusters of Starved Rock State Park in Illinois, William B. Umstead Park in North Carolina, or S. B. Elliot Park in northwestern Pennsylvania are steeped in the aspirations of the New Deal decade.

Like parkways and regional parks, state parks predated the Depression. The first few appeared as early as the 1880s, but the concept was not fully developed until after World War I.[1] Parks Commissioner Robert Moses and landscape architects John Nolen and Frederick Law Olmsted, Jr., all central figures in the landscape planning of the New Deal, influenced the early direction of the state park. By the close of the 1920s Iowa, Wisconsin, Indiana,

New York, and Connecticut had already established strong park systems.[2] In addition, South Dakota's Custer State Park, Minnesota's Itasco Park and New York's Palisades Park had pioneered the pattern of rough-cut stone, crude timbers, and wooded demesne that would identify almost all state and national park work of the thirties. As with other recreation landscape development, the outlines already existed, but the New Deal fleshed out the final form and details and set standards that would persist for years.

The Depression landscape styles dominated, if not in artistic excellence, in numbers. The state park was an especially popular item. It provided an ideal staging ground for the Civilian Conservation Corps, which worked mainly on state parks in every part of the nation but the West. By the end of the decade state park acreage had doubled; the number of parks had increased by more than 30 percent, and five states had created their first park. Inspired by the sight of so much diligent and gratuitous industry on the part of the CCC, twenty-one states that had not already done so hastened to set up state park administrations.[3] The plaque attached to the lodge at Starved Rock State Park asserts that the CCC advanced Illinois's state park movement by fifty years. That plaque could justifiably adorn the lodge of almost any state park.

The state park drew from the long-established resort traditions of the United States. Using the example of the North Woods—the Adirondack Great Camps and New England summer spas—the woodland retreat was popularized in the state park. One of the earliest mountain resorts, at Asheville, North Carolina, illustrates this process of democratization. The curtain opens on the Vanderbilts, who built the palatial Biltmore House in 1890. In 1913, the opening of the rambling Grove Park Inn lured the well-heeled bourgeoisie. Tourism burgeoned. By the thirties, a handful of trailer courts and tourist homes serviced those at the lower end of the economic spectrum. Although shabbily equipped, these cheap accommodations were popular, because Asheville alone of the resorts in the Southern Highlands offered a variety of tourist facilities.[4] With the New Deal, the public arrived. Campers traveling on the unfinished Blue Ridge Parkway could now pitch their tents at the newly opened waysides along the parkway or at the nearby CCC overnight shelter in Mt. Mitchell State Park. These alternatives were even more modest than accommodations in the gardener's cottage on the Vanderbilt estate, but they represented the vanguard of the democratization of summer vacation.

By the time FDR and his forces entered the picture, the lower classes were spilling onto the holiday preserves of the haut monde; Frederick Law Olmsted, Jr. had submitted his guidelines for the selection of state park land in California; and Robert Moses held full command over an advanced system of some sixty state parks in New York. Despite these developments, debate over the nature and purpose of the state park was still raging. The National Park Service viewed the state park as a buffer deflecting rabid recreation-seekers from the more tranquil and inviolate reaches of its territory. Toward this end the NPS promoted state parks by initiating the first National Conference on State Parks in 1921. Harold Ickes was carrying on the same protectionist attitude in 1935 when he inveighed against the construction of artificial lakes except in state parks. In support of this idea Robert Moses endorsed an active role for state parks. He insisted that no state park would succeed without a swimming area.[5] Moses had the personality and power to institute his ideas, as the subsequent proliferation of lakes in state parks all over the country suggests.

The main opposition to the view of state parks promoted by Moses and the National Park Service arose from the landscape architecture profession, which had long been restless to break from its customary round of private estates, subdivisions, university grounds, and the occasional city park. The landscape architecture literature of the 1920s was full of advice and criticism concerning the state park movement. Nolen and Olmsted had made direct theoretical contributions, but on the whole, as Frank Waugh pointed out, state and national park planning had not involved landscape expertise.[6] But the Depression ended this exclusion.

By their entry into the domain of the state park, landscape architects converted what had been largely a creature of chance into a synthesis of orderly design. The participation of landscape architects allowed a balance to be struck between the people's desire, on the one hand, for active games and, on the other, for the wilds. Swimming areas (with a bow to Moses) became almost standard, but the facilities deferred to the woodland vision.

The CCC, most instrumental in spreading the state park vision, transformed unlikely and downright inhospitable settings across the land into vignettes evocative of the Eastern woodland resort. Just such a setpiece emerged in the late 1930s on the treeless plains of northwestern Kansas. Out of the buffalo grass rose a picturesque stone building, a lake, and a sheltering grove of trees (fig. 51). One of several lakes installed in Kansas by the WPA and CCC, this fragment of a forest offered the basics of a scenario that was being duplicated from the Berkshires to the Big Bend.

A Depression-built state park might be as simple as Sappa Creek, which was essentially a wayside with picnicking, swimming, and shelter. A single structure, like the recreation hall at Russian Gulch on California's northern coast or the observation tower on the summit of Mt. Mitchell in North Carolina, might complement a basic scheme of hiking, picnicking, and camping. A few cabins might be scattered through the woods, as at Pennsylvania's S. B. Elliot Park, or perched beside a lake, as at Daingerfield State Park in East Texas. The apparent naturalness of the settings obscures the fact that the New Deal state park was often an elaborate artifice created out of very little. At S. B. Elliot and Sappa Creek the trees were imported. At Daingerfield and Sappa Creek workmen dug the lakes. Hence, the very trees and waters of many thirties state parks represent a sizeable investment of manpower. Ohio's Blue

51. *Sappa Creek State Lake, Oberlin, Kansas, Recreation hall, 1938.*

Rock State Park boasts swimming, boating, fishing, and waterside picnicking because the CCC spent several years constructing Cutler Lake with horses and drags. Cutler Lake is one of over seventy-five such lakes gouged by the glacier of government work relief. The most ambitious lake is found in Louisiana, where the brigades of unemployed excavated a two thousand-acre water hole for Chicot State Park. Like the playground in the city, the state park popped up in the countryside, a ready-made respite for both rural and urban residents.

Even the seemingly basic overnight cabin dates almost exclusively from the Depression. California, Pennsylvania, Ohio, New York, and most other states have long since stopped building the cozy individual units which accommodate from two to six people and offer kitchen facilities and/or stove and fireplace (figs. 52, 53). In Pennsylvania, a statewide lottery is held three times a year to raffle reservations for its 146 Depression-era cabins. During the busy summer months, North Carolina imposes a minimum stay of one week and a maximum of two weeks in its rustic cabins. Only in the Southeast has cabin-building continued.

During the Depression the overnight cabin was just another facility in a state park that might well include a lake or two, a beach, a boathouse, a golf course, trails, picnic areas, shelter houses, an observation tower, a lodge, and perhaps even a historic site. The most elaborate state parks, which included all these facilities, were built, for two reasons, in Texas and Oklahoma. First, these states basked in the double boon of newly discovered oil and federal

52. *Green Lakes State Park, New York State, cabin.*

53. *Bastrop State Park, Texas, Cabin.*

funding. Second, Herb Maier, a trend-setting architect, was for a time the regional officer in charge of building in this area. During this period Oklahoma built its first six state parks, and stocked them all with cabins and lakes. Texas, which had a good head start, elaborated even further. MacKenzie State Park boasted a bathhouse, an athletic clubhouse, and a polo field. The attention lavished upon the best of the CCC state parks encompassed even the furnishings. At Bastrop State Park, a pleasant pine oasis near Austin, a cowboy bas relief, a suspended wagon wheel, and handcrafted furniture greeted visitors to the main lodge (fig. 54). Outstanding for their craftsmanship and completeness, Texas's and Oklahoma's state parks exemplify luxury that during the New Deal was usually forsaken in favor of quantity.

Pared-down descendants of munificent, turn-of-the-century Adirondack camps and grandiose park lodges, Depression structures like the lodge of Petit Jean in the Ozarks honored both the lore and the lay of the land (fig. 55).

54. *Bastrop State Park, Texas, interior of lodge.*

55. *Petit Jean State Park, Arkansas, lodge.*

The buildings look more like the earth and trees that surround them than the lodges, bathhouses, cabins, and shelters they really are. Looking at the rough wood bathhouse in Green Lakes State Park outside Syracuse, New York, one can easily picture a buckskin-clad hunter inside frying squirrel for supper (fig. 56). These recreation shelters invoke both the land and its earliest occupants. The rounded arches, "belfry," "apse," and "stone" (in fact caliche) of the dining hall at Lake Corpus Christi State Park seem to beckon the proselytizing Franciscan friar, not the vacationing mechanic, to dinner (fig. 57). Romantic evocations of an earlier age, these pioneer dwellings encircle the man-made ponds of Depression America in much the same way that Roman *tempiettas* dot the artificial lakes of eighteenth-century English private parks.

The state parks that most reflect the ideals of the thirties began life not as state parks, but rather as Recreation Demonstration Areas (RDAs). Devised by the Resettlement Administration, RDAs made possible the conversion of large tracts of depleted agricultural land into prototypical state parks. The federal government, through the Resettlement Administration and later the National Parks Service, promoted the idea of creating model camping and recreational complexes that would cater primarily to the poor and handicapped. After development, the RDAs were to be restored to the states.

Conceived as "training grounds" to acquaint the underprivileged with the joys of the woods, these oddities passed into general use in various ways. Twenty-nine of the original forty-six eventually became state parks; twelve were waysides along the Blue Ridge Parkway. The remainder merged into

56. *Green Lakes State Park, New York State, lake and bathhouse, 1972.*

existing national parks or monuments. (See Appendix for the complete list of Recreation Demonstration Areas.) One out of the forty-six rose to stardom—called Shangri-la during the Roosevelt administration, it was later renamed Camp David.

Roosevelt's view, shared by Rexford Tugwell, Assistant Secretary of Agriculture then head of the Resettlement Administration, held that agriculture on submarginal land is regressive. Because the land is not productive enough, farmers cannot maintain an adequate standard of living and thus require costly social services. Roosevelt believed that it would be more appropriate to convert the land to forest—trees being a favorite New Deal cure-all. The force of this thesis converted four hundred thousand acres into Recreation Demonstration land.

A typical representative of this site conversion program was the Crabtree Creek Recreation Demonstration Area midway between Raleigh and Durham in North Carolina. Two lakes, several scenic streams, extensive pine forest, and ample group camps were hewn from fifteen thousand acres of worn-out cotton-growing land pockmarked by abandoned houses (figs. 58, 59). The Resettlement Administration's eligibility report described one tract of ten thousand acres that supported only forty-six families. Actually, the land only maintained thirty-two families—fourteen were on relief. Adverse agricultural practices—poor cultivation, sharecropping, merchant credit farming, and, after the Civil War, one-crop production—had brought this Piedmont land to

57. *Lake Corpus Christi State Park, Texas, refectory.*

58. *William B. Umstead State Park, North Carolina, group camp cabins.*

59. *William B. Umstead State Park, North Carolina, shower house.*

its knees.[7] Today the site, reduced to two-thirds its former size and re-christened William B. Umstead State Park, hosts, in place of cotton, swim-mers, campers, and picnickers galore.

One of only two RDAs built on the West Coast, the Mendocino Wood-lands aspired to an ideal of group living in the wilds drawn from the distant Indian past. Located 130 miles north of San Francisco in thinly populated, remote countryside near the coast, the Woodlands was a giant challenge to build. Good labor was scarce enough without the added stipulation that 90 percent had to come from the relief rolls. The elaborate orchestration and planning of the Woodlands demonstrates the serious care lavished on these projects. Two duplicate, oversized portfolios still in the hands of the National Park Service in San Francisco reveal many sheets of detailed plans prefaced by pages of photos of the area before development. From one of these sets comes the plan for the "Family Vacation Area," a complete assemblage that includes a dining lodge, twenty-four camper cabins, eight leader cabins, an infirmary, help and staff quarters, a recreation hall, and campfire circle (fig. 60). In addition, the planting of pines and the digging of a lake guaranteed the era's

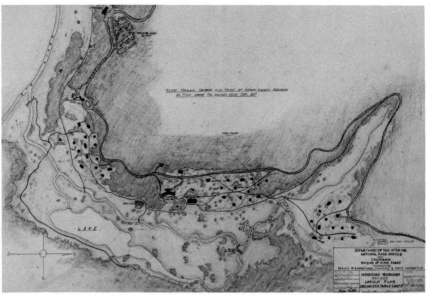

60. *Mendocino Woodlands, California, Organized Family Camp plan, 1936.*

quintessential therapeutic environment. The Mendocino Woodlands aptly combines the two New Deal aspirations of communion with nature and frater-nal cooperation.

Within just twenty miles of the population centers of Richmond, Pe-tersburg, and Hopewell in Virginia, the Swift Creek RDA, now Pocahontas State Park, subscribed more convincingly to the stated intent of serving the disadvantaged and handicapped. When it first opened, the same summer as the Woodlands, it offered on the site of former tobacco plantations three new lakes, numerous buildings, and miles of roads. From July to September of that first summer, one hundred thousand people took advantage of the extensive facilities, which included camping for nearly two hundred, child-care, a nature and crafts center, swimming lessons, games, and equipment supervised by recreation leaders. On the beach a piano sat on a sheltered platform. After a day of revel at Swift Creek, one grateful visitor wrote to a Richmond paper words that summarized the intention behind the RDAs and much else created in the recreation splurge of the thirties: "Most such places, you know," the satisfied citizen noted, "are for people who have plenty of time and money to enjoy them. But Swift Creek is convenient to a lot of us who couldn't go any other place."[8]

To reinforce its goal of educating the poor about woods and recreation, from 1938 to 1940 Washington undertook various "Program Demonstrations" in state parks and RDAs around the country. Supervised games, piano playing, and child-care were among forty-one activities offered at Swift Creek in Vir-ginia as part of a special training session. An even more rural and remote state park in Mississippi offers the most touching evidence of the idealistic fervor which accompanied the education effort. Mrs. C. V. Gross, a researcher connected with the program, described the area, with an Eleanor Roosevelt prudishness popular at the time, as backward and poor, the only organized entertainment being "undesirable commercial amusement enterprises such as roadhouses and poolhalls."[9] She detailed a hard, unremitting life of chores, from which Sunday offered release only for men and boys. Women and girls ended the week with extra cooking and dishwashing. To these burdened people the three recreation leaders at Percy Quinn State Park brought swimming instruction, dancing, ping-pong, croquet, and shuffleboard—second only to swimming in popularity. Although the summer's program was not revolutionary enough to induce little girls into bathing suits, it did introduce a backwater to life, particularly to recreation, which was increasingly a design feature of Western living.

The same altruistic hopes that produced legions of WPA playgrounds suffused the state parks and Recreation Demonstration Areas. Cooperative play was presumed to lead to a better society. Contact with nature would enhance the benefits to be gained from wholesome outdoor pastimes. In the Depression era, nature was seen as a moral force, but one sometimes relegated to a mere background against which games and other activities took place. Today nature, rather than recreation, plays the dominant role. Such popular modern preoccupations as rafting, skydiving, and backpacking pit the adventurous against the vagaries of nature. Less strenuous sports like jogging still involve individual rather than group prowess. The intricate athletic equipment of the contemporary playground acclimates children to the more individualistic standards of our own time. The group camps, baseball diamonds, horseshoe pits, and other comparatively tame paraphernalia of the thirties oriented the young more toward a cooperative spirit.

The loss of self which is the goal of recreational experience today is the product of stretching the senses and the body to their limits. Less familiar to current generations is the facility with which people a few decades ago could organize group activities and immerse themselves in history. If parkways meandered into the past, state parks and RDAs also conjured up a departed age. The Demonstration Areas combined Indian-style clustered camps with pioneer construction; state parks invoked the pioneer vision with artifacts, ruins, and reconstructions. As temples and ruins embodied the "classic" theme of the eighteenth-century English landscape garden, so forts, Indian villages, authentic log cabins, and, in Spring Mill State Park in Indiana, an entire early nineteenth-century village colorfully evoked the pioneer theme of the Depression-era American state park. Harold Ickes summarized the role of parks and their involvement with history:

In the wilderness beauties of our national monuments, we have living pictures of the great past of our country, landmarks to show the road we have travelled and to point out the path that leads into the future. In these areas and in the growing numbers of

State, county and municipal parks throughout the Nation, we give our people unique and happy fortifications against unrest and war.[10]

This view of parks as "living pictures of the great past" contrasts markedly with the modern attitude that parks are ecological preserves. Because the dominant history and culture was that of the forested East, that landscape spread West as the landscape of leisure. By the fifties and sixties the desire for a symbolic landscape had faded; the West had come into its own and a more purist, scientific approach toward the land predominated. The deterioration of many CCC-built landscapes accompanied this shift of attitude. Plants and debris have choked the lake at the Mendocino Woodlands almost to extinction. Overgrown and unthinned tree stands block out the sun, casting the park into gloomy shadow. In Kansas, Sappa Creek State Lake was sold off, so that the dam attributed to the WPA by a metal plaque now holds back not a lake but a field of wheat (fig. 61).

Down the road from Sappa Creek a new state park inaugurated in the 1960s dramatizes the changes in perception during the last quarter of a century. The very name—Prairie Dog State Park—signals a philosophic revolution. The forest has receded; the prairie is not only accepted, but embraced. In place of trees, plastic umbrellas offer relief from the sun; the few token trees only serve to reinforce the omnipresent reality of the prairie (fig. 62). In place of the stone pioneer hut, a functional, boxy brick building offers a reduced list

61. *Former Sappa Creek State Lake, Kansas, commemorative marker.*

62. *Prairie Dog State Park, Kansas, 1972.*

of facilities. All that remains from the classic state park plan is Prairie Dog Lake, an artifice alien to the creatures for which it was named. Variations on Prairie Dog State Park proliferated throughout the Midwest and Plains areas in the era following World War II. Economics accounts to a certain extent for the bareness of Prairie Dog in comparison to Sappa Creek. The Depression era was truly a period of plenty for parks. The money released a yearning for the past that expressed itself in the fashioning of pioneer worlds.

As testimony to that spirit, witness the building of a cut-stone boathouse in the metropolitan park of Perry, Oklahoma. Carroll P. Graves, in his youth a CCC recruit, recounts the effort involved in laying the immense steps that lead from the boathouse to the landing (fig. 63). The steps were composed of red sandstone slabs 8 feet long and 12 or 16 inches in width. Still greater effort went into the raising of the roof for the men's room. This roof consisted of a single 8-inch-thick slab measuring 10 by 12 feet. According to Mr. Graves, the hoisting of this rock required the services of 20 peeled and greased blackjack poles, a log chain, 100 feet of 20-inch-thick Navy rope, a tractor, 4 Chevrolet trucks—and, he forgets to add, the backup support of a CCC camp of 200 men.[11] Such gargantuan effort refutes the contentions that native raw building materials were used simply because they were cheap and available, or because the rustic style of building best utilized the ubiquitous surplus of hand labor. A force stronger than economics dictated these Herculean labors. From parkway to state park to boathouse the urge to recapture a romanticized past precipitated the outstanding achievements of the period.

A fusion of nostalgia and economics propagated Government Rustic.

63. *Perry Lake Metropolitan Park Boathouse, Perry, Oklahoma.*

The federal government provided the labor and, after 1936, the design staff; local entities had only to provide materials. Indigenous stone and wood were readily available. The labor pool would also likely include workers who knew how to cope a log (shape the end to fit with a supporting member). Subsequently an infestation of masonry outhouses and rough lumber shelters settled over the land, from the gatehouse to Fairmount Park in Philadelphia to the Tuolomne Meadows Comfort Station at Yosemite.

Frank Waugh elucidated the rustic style at the outset of the building splurge in 1933. He proclaimed that the building should "fit the ground," that foundations be deemphasized, that plantings be native and as naturalistic as possible, and, most important, that all ornament be forbidden.[12]

Some of these commandments ruling government park work appeared simultaneously in the buildings and writings of the era's most celebrated designer. "Architecture which is really architecture proceeds from the ground," wrote Frank Lloyd Wright, who extolled simplicity and abhorred ornament not intrinsic to materials.[13] At the same time as the CCC and WPA were constructing their log and stone fantasies, Wright was experimenting with prototype mass housing and building Fallingwater, his most noted residence (fig. 64). Wright's domain—domestic architecture—and his materials— brick, concrete, cut stone, and milled wood—differed from the subject and manner of Government Rustic; nor does the dramatic, highly personalized Fallingwater ressemble the conventional, subdued structures of the CCC and WPA. Yet the Chicago renegade and the Government Rustic designers shared a ground-hugging regard for nature. The two crossing, cantilevered balconies

64. *Frank Lloyd Wright's "Fallingwater," Pennsylvania, rendered perspective.*

reiterate the double-rock ledge of the falls. The falls almost seem to spring from the house itself. Wright tied his building tightly to the ground. And like the followers of the rustic mode, he eschewed formal planting and elaborate gardens that might weaken that tie. Government Rustic and Frank Lloyd Wright alike were seeking an indigenous architecture free of Old World dictates. Beyond these similarities, the structures spawned by these two disparate sources reflect the purposefulness of an architecture in service to a cause.

In 1923, just about the time Wright moved to Los Angeles, the National Park Service's Branch of Planning and Design was transferred there from Yosemite. Purportedly, Tom Vint, head of the Park Service office, met and worked briefly with the Chicago architect.[14] Nor is such a meeting unlikely. Although one drew from the woods and the other from the plains, both schools of building celebrated America.

Besides patriotism a common background united the National Park Service and Frank Lloyd Wright. Both emerged from the Arts and Crafts movement of England of the second half of the nineteenth century. Led by John Ruskin and William Morris, the movement glorified manual labor, particularly highly individualized work which rejected conventions of design and ornament. Their ideas quickly took root in American soils prepared by the transcendental teachings of Emerson and Thoreau, and in the late 1880s produced the shingle and rubblestone residences extolled by Vincent Scully in *The Shingle Style and the Stick Style.*

On the literary end, Gustav Stickley's magazine *The Craftsman* best presented the sentiment of this romantic current which saw nature as the true fount of inspiration. From 1902 to 1932 it preached the unity of land and building, and the treatment of ornament as an integral part of an interior. Wilhelm Miller, influential editor and author in 1915 of *The Prairie School of Landscape Architecture,* also hailed the native landscape and handcraftsmanship. These themes of naturalism later made their way into the writings of both Frank Lloyd Wright and the makers of Government Rustic.

Wright's often-stated fascination with machines, however, qualified his sympathy with the Arts and Crafts cause. He thought that properly used the machine was beneficial. By the twenties, urban architecture at large paid homage to the wonders of technology. Streamlined buildings mimicked ships, automobiles, and later airplanes. This architectural infatuation with speed became America's *moderne.* [15] The urban building of the Depression made overtures to the moderne, but the rural parks held fast to the tradition of Ruskin and Morris, Americanized with a hearty dose of Crockett and Boone.

Excellently suited to the alleviation of extreme unemployment, the rustic style occupied thousands of otherwise idle hands with chopping, hauling, sawing, and chiseling. As adverse economic conditions persisted, hand-hewn log and stone structures flourished throughout the nation's woodlands. Orchestrating the various creative currents, landscape architects shaped the final products according to the current definition of their profession as "the art

65. *Norris State Resort Park, Tennessee, cabins built in 1933. Drawing by Madelaine Gill Linden.*

of land use for the maximum human use, convenience, and enjoyment, with a controlling guard for beauty."[16]

The distinctive purity of this style stands out in comparison with the recently developed "state resort parks," which can be found in Tennessee, Kentucky, and Alabama. Norris Dam State Resort Park in East Tennessee consists of two separate segments, a section on the east side of Norris Lake built by the CCC, and a modern complex, completed in 1976, on the west side. The older section offers the cabins, community building, picnic grounds, and amphitheater endemic to the public vacation grounds of the Depression era. The facilities huddle together on a hill above the lake (fig. 65). Out of sight of the lake, the modern recreation grouping boasts nine three-bedroom deluxe cabins complete with air conditioning (fig. 66). A multiservice complex incongruously called the "Village Green" harbors a laundromat, store, snack bar, Olympic-sized pool, and a playground which is finished, as are all the buildings, in sleek gray boards. The unadorned, exaggerated angularity of this 1970s vacation cluster descends in a direct line from Charles Moore's 1965 Northern California resort Sea Ranch, and the comfort and convenience clash loudly with the rustic style of the shingled ensemble on the east side.

The modern complex is processed, a step or three more removed from nature than the thirties campground. A concrete pool, air-conditioning, and a snack bar replace the lake, breezes, and barbecue pit, while the playground usurps the imaginative potential of trees and concealing shrubs. Norris Dam Resort Park is not an isolated case; "processed" design appears all too fre-

66. *Norris State Resort Park, Tennessee, cabins built in 1976. Drawing by Madelaine Gill Linden.*

quently in contemporary versions of ex-urban park facilities. The modern emphasis on ecology stresses empirical observation of nature, but simultaneously "land management" policies prescribe the minimum amount of human intervention. Together sophisticated facilities and hands-off attitudes secure the viewer behind a picture window. In defense of the New Deal's brash meddling with nature, escapees from this architectural refinement can still enjoy the plain beauty of Depression-era state park land.

CHAPTER SIX

The Landscape Profession
in the Depression

THE DEPRESSION disoriented the nation. The economic reversal and, later, government counteraction pried people from their niches and scattered them across the land. The exodus of three hundred thousand Okies to the West Coast was the most notorious of the dislocations. All over the country similar displacements occurred. Kentucky farmboys were shipped to the canyons of Utah; street toughs from Hoboken and the Bronx ended up in the wilds of Wyoming in company with naval commanders from Pensacola and landscape architects from the University of Iowa and Cornell. For New Yorkers in Yellowstone who complained that they thought they were going to a park but could only see trees, for landscape architects who expected to execute formal gardens and schools in the suburbs but ended by installing comfort stations and parking lots in the redwoods, the Depression brought not bankruptcy and ruin, but education and unexpected opportunity.

Less well-known than the dispersal from the nation's plains was the infiltration of its woods and canyons. This was a movement of adherents to, not refugees from, nature. A rising tide of nature-seeking vacationers was followed by a swell of developers working in the name of conservation. This last influx of CCC workers also bore the landscape architects.

Mass tourist migration was a new phenomenon in the United States. Prior to the 1920s, when the automobile turned from luxury to locust, the problem of recreation had been largely one solved by containing people in one spot, whether it be a playground, a playing field, a zoo, or a botanical garden. With the onslaught of the automobile, it became necessary to provide for a population both liberated from long hours of work and newly mobilized. Cities flung out parks and parkways; states cordoned off outlying lands to placate the more adventurous; but still the holiday migrants kept going. By the 1930s a number had reached the Tennessee Valley, where planners anxiously analyzed the situation: "A generation ago vacationists still sat on the front porches of resort hotels all summer long and enjoyed a static holiday. Today they move, they investigate, they mingle. Whether for better or for worse, the automobiles and improved roads have made possible a mobile type of vacation which has proved immensely popular."[1]

By 1936 the volume of visitors in the national and state forests swelled to ten times what it had been in 1916. National parks reported that tourism had doubled between 1936 and 1937. "Until recently," noted the United States Forest Service, "few people except hunters and fishermen went to the woods for recreation."[2] The Forest Service was dumbfounded. Its charter didn't even mention recreation as a legitimate function. Congress had begun allocating a small amount of money to the USFS for recreation purposes only in 1922. The National Park Service, which by definition had been in the tourist business since its inception in 1916, was somewhat more prepared. Some of its parks, such as Yellowstone and Yosemite, had been welcoming the carriage and train trade since the second half of the nineteenth century. And the year before the inception of the National Emergency Works Program, the Park Service had prepared plans for its twenty-two parks in anticipation of receiving some funds.

Despite these preliminary motions on the part of the Park Service, neither service had much contact with landscape architects. When Frank Waugh complained that few landscape architects had ever received a commission from either state or national parks, he could also have added national forests to the list. He did not because he was one of only three landscape architects associated with the Forest Service in the almost thirty years from its inception in 1905 to 1933. But at the outset of the CCC program, the Forest Service had not one landscape architect in its employ; the Park Service had only ten on its payroll.[3] The advent of the CCC rapidly changed this situation. By mid-June, only two and a half months after the enabling legislation was approved, 1,300 camps had been set up.[4] By the fall the Forest Service was home for 1,265 camps; 175 more had been assigned to parks. Both the NPS and USFS had begun the hunt which was to propel the profession of landscape architecture out of obscurity.[5] Elated, the members of this profession came to conclude that "in connection with the Government's emergency expenditures, probably no other profession has had a greater demand for its services." The Park Service instituted a policy of hiring a landscape architect for each camp.[6] The migration of the landscape architect from the clipped boxwood to the wide-open spaces had begun.

The frenzy reached its zenith between 1935 and 1936. The CCC now sponsored 2,600 camps, and the National Park Service hired 100 additional landscape architects, architects, and engineers, bringing its total to 220. The Forest Service, at last galvanized into action, took the radical step of hiring a landscape architect for its Washington office. Also, having earlier dismissed the profession as a "bunch of esthetes and idealists," the Forest Service plucked Albert Taylor from the top of the American Society of Landscape Architects and assigned him the task of evaluating the CCC's performance.[7]

The Park Service and Forestry were pursuing the graduates of landscaping programs before they had doffed their caps and gowns. Former national parks recruiter William Carnes recalls snatching them up "without even a picture" and boasted that the NPS employed 400 landscape architects.[8] Even assuming that the students hadn't had a chance yet to join the professional organization, that number must be inflated, since the Society listed a membership, as of 1933, of only 284 people.

Albert Taylor's contention that 90 percent of the landscaping profession was in the employ of the government rings true. Sanford Hill claims that the unprecedented demand created a substantial number of "instant" landscape architects.[9] Without the intervention of the Depression, out of the 90 percent only a small number would have opted for public employment. The rare few who had joined the Park Service before the Depression were mostly natives of the western states. They included Tom Vint, head of the Branch of Plans and Designs, from Utah and California, and Bill Carnes, Vint's assistant, who claims he was the first landscape architect ever to hail from Montana. Most landscape architects followed the example of Darcy Bonnet and Sanford Hill. Whether from the Midwest, as was Hill, or from the East Coast, like Bonnet, they gravitated to New York City and were employed by one of its thriving private firms, such as Vitale and Geiffert or Brinkley and Holbrook. In these offices they mastered the intricacies of designing for private estates, institutions, and the occasional park. But with the onset of the Depression these jobs vanished. Sanford Hill and Darcy Bonnet were thrown out into the lengthening lines at the automat along with "some of the best designers in New York," according to Hill. Between 1928 and 1932 the number of architectural contracts plummeted 86 percent, and for those in line at the automat the prospects for reemployment in architecture and related fields began to look increasingly dim.[10] Darcy Bonnet recalls watching a family sell the magnolia out of their front yard.

Sanford Hill returned to his native Iowa and found a job supervising the CCC at Backbone State Park. Darcy Bonnet became a project leader at the CCC campgrounds in the Monongahela National Forest in West Virginia. Both remained in government service for the next forty years.

Landscape architects and the government were both surprised at their productive relationship. Before and even during the Roosevelt administration, a sizeable amount of suspicion existed between the two. In 1926, at the age of 27, Charles Eliot II had acquired the position of Director of National Capitol Park and Planning because, in his own words, "everyone else turned it down."[11] When prosperity began to return in 1936, Darcy Bonnet's former boss in New York urged him to return to do some "honest work." And the Forest Service had long resisted hiring landscape architects because it viewed them as impractical.

When landscape architects went to work an masse for the federal government, they learned large-scale design and planning, administrative skills, and how to deal with a wide variety of people. For example, in the 1930s Tom Vint instituted the master plan, which has become a stock-in-trade of landscape architecture, as a method of creating development criteria for the national parks.[12] In turn, the NPS and USFS gained a cadre of personnel thoroughly trained by the intensive charette of the Roosevelt decade. When these caretaker organizations initiated a new round of construction in the late fifties, the men who had paced out the first parking lots and routed the original trails coordinated the campaign.

The development of public lands drew landscape architects out of Boston and New York into the Appalachians and over the Mississippi. Although a few native Californian landscape architects worked in Los Angeles and San Francisco, imported professionals from the East mastermined the major developments. For example, Olmsted Brothers out of Boston designed the exclusive subdivision of Palos Verdes in 1923. But East Coast landscape architects often had to be prodded to move west from their Boston and New York haunts. Darcy Bonnet discovered this when he tried to find someone to be the regional landscape architect for California and ended up having to take the job himself. The Depression provided that westward impetus, and changed the demography of job opportunity. Since most CCC camps were in national forests and national parks, the job openings lay westward. Thus, when the subdivision work dried up, landscape architect George Gibbs filled in the time with a variety of public work—a report on Kings Canyon, an administrative post supervising CCC camps in seven Western states, and the projected design of a polo field for Berkeley's Tilden Park.[13] The Depression helped landscape architects discover their country, and many from the East or Midwest are now happily retired among the golden hills they discovered upon arriving in California during hard times.

The westward migration of designers promoted the gradual elevation of this continent over "the Continent." Previously, Harvard had fixed the standard for design, which was largely an American translation of the European tradition. During the 1930s, landscape architects from outside the establishment, and later from within it, began to challenge the Harvard hegemony. Comments by two landscape architects who rose to prominence with the New Deal plainly express this resentment. Bill Carnes crowed that when the Depression hit, his colleagues from Iowa State were "more ready to go to work" and "less interested in breeding dogs and private summer camps" than were their Harvard equivalents. Conrad Wirth insists that the American Society of Landscape Architects barred Frank Waugh from membership because he

wasn't a graduate of Harvard.[14] Accurate or not, these statements are revealing of the sentiment of the times. The Depression undermined Harvard's
privilege because demand was oblivious to the source of the supply, and as a
result graduates of more obscure schools were finally able to hack their way out
of the nation's woods into positions of prominence. Moreover, the less established schools were quicker than Harvard to tailor their curriculum to reflect
the new demands. By 1934 Iowa State University was offering an option in
park design. Signaled by such changes, the 1930s saw the transition from
private to public patronage and a continental drift west of the innovative
spirit.

In 1931 Henry Hubbard, editor of Landscape Architecture, trumpeted
these prophetic words:

We now think of ourselves as a force worth considering in the affairs of the country.
We believe that we have opportunities of which we have not as yet availed ourselves,
duties which we have not as yet performed. We are willing to spend time and money in
order to begin our honest part in many matters not local and emphatically not
confined within the boundaries of the garden or of the private estate.[15]

Within three years of this pronouncement, 90 percent of his colleagues had
vaulted the garden wall. Men like Phelps Wyman, who before the Depression
was a land planner for Minneapolis and Milwaukee with an extensive practice
throughout the Midwest, and Wilbur Cook, who had been resident dean of the
profession in Los Angeles and subdivision designer for a large segment of
Beverly Hills, were grateful to bear the modest title of Landscape Foreman and
to be on the federal payroll. Perhaps Hubbard could not have imagined how far
from the garden or private estate the landscape architect would actually travel.

Although Phelps Wyman remained in Milwaukee planting and classify-
ing plants for Whitnall Park and the Boerner Botanical Garden, Wilbur Cook
found himself deep in the forests of Sequoia National Park. Wyman's assign-
ment, as lowly as it may have been, was not an unfamiliar variation on
previous work. Wilbur Cook, however, confronted a jumble of tasks ranging
from the building of skating facilities to the improvement of roads, trails, and
grounds around buildings. Toboggan trails and skating facilities were a long
sight from Hollywood swimming pools and Beverly Hills subdivisions. As
Darcy Bonnet recalled, "Most landscape architects hadn't messed around with
public recreation."[16]

Foremen such as Cook and Wyman were on the lowest rung of the
Emergency Conservation Works bureaucracy, but they anchored the whole
makeshift structure. Without qualified foremen some landscape architects
were reluctant to undertake projects. For example, Ernest Davidson, writing
from Mt. Rainier in 1934, advised against using the CCC for capital improvements such as structures and minor roads because of a lack of skilled supervision.[17] Philip Elwood, an inspector for the State Park program, confronted the
same problem in his area. Reporting from the Great Plains, he complained of

"low standards of construction, particularly in the wide variety of work done by CCC labor," a state of affairs he attributed partially to lack of interest on part of the enrollees, but largely to the dearth of skilled direction.[18]

Competent leadership was the most single critical factor in the whole Emergency Works program. Good foremen, as reported by landscape architect Melvin Borgeson from New Jersey's state parks and forests, afforded "splendid results."[19] Throughout the thirties the presence of experienced professionals like Borgeson, Cook, and Wyman in the field explains why contemporary park officials so greatly respect the work done during the New Deal decade.

In part because they underestimated the leadership potential, the organizers of the CCC at first did not envision the corps as much more than a giant maintenance and forestry crew. Although the legislation spoke ambiguously of the CCC engaging in an "orderly program of useful public works," the skills required for rustic architecture were considered too complex for the recruits.[20] Moreover, the Public Works Administration was already engaged in a major construction program in the national parks. Consequently, for the first year or two the CCC engaged primarily in reforestation, flood control, and rudimentary construction work like roads and trails.[21] But gradually, under the direction of trained designers and engineers, the role of the Tree Army expanded beyond basic forestry assignments. Reports of successful CCC building projects percolated in from Sequoia, Rainier, Glacier, and other parks. Ernest Davidson, who had advised against using the CCC for capital improvements, three years later praised the corps for its construction work. By 1938 CCC projects at Sequoia progressed from repairs and improvements to the construction of a residence and an equipment shed.

The alarmed response of the Forest Service confirms the great progress made by the CCC in the national and state parks. Having once dismissed landscape architects as "esthetes and idealists," the Forest Service now took note of the work being done by its rival, the NPS, and feared that its own more basic improvements "were going to suffer by comparison."[22] This led to the startling reversal of policy under which Forestry induced Albert Taylor into its services.

Yellowstone, Backbone, and the Monongahela were a long way from Palos Verdes, but the future for landscape architects lay with public projects, not with munificent estates and lush subdivisions. The transition was sometimes as rough as a first mule ride down the Grand Canyon. (What's more, the disgruntled park superintendent, feeling upstaged, might have been secretly hoping for the mule to bolt.[23]) But despite the obstacles, a swimming pool and a lodge appeared on the floor of the Grand Canyon in tandem with unexpected amenities in untoward places all across the land. Likewise, landscape architects popped up in hitherto incongruous spots—and stayed on.

In fact, the defection of the landscape architect to the public sphere for a time caused the private garden to fall into a sorry and neglected state. The emphasis on public parks, forests, and highways for a long time obscured small-scale ventures. Art on a large scale and simplified for mass production submerged the spirit of the eclectic and the fine sense of detailing and proportion that occupied the pre-Depression design world. But today architects have been recalling Palladio, Robert Trent Jones, and McKim, Mead and White. Landscape architects are revisiting the Villa Lante, the Spanish pool, and the English garden gate. In true cyclical fashion the formal garden is making a comeback. Italian gardens are again emblazoning the pages of the profession's journals. Young landscape architects are designing postmodern box gardens and water ramps. Formal compositions like New York's Conservatory Garden are undergoing a revival, as are the gardenesque and the nineteenth-century English garden designer Getrude Jekyll. Landscape architecture is again being explored as a "fine art."

As for the landscape architects themselves, their prestige and importance is obviously not bound to the same cyclical path as the formal garden. The land designers' influence skyrocketed with the Great Depression but appears to have ended with it too. Short of another market collapse, only a radical change in social outlook could restore the brief triumph experienced by the landscape architect between 1933 and 1941.

CHAPTER SEVEN

Nothing So American: The National Parks and Forests

D URING THE 1930s the forests and plains were the setting for an extraordinary convocation of landscape architects, architects, government officials, soldiers, and indigent youth. These individuals often entered the woods in ignorance, but a common vision of America unified their purpose. To landscape architect and soldier alike the great American nature preserves symbolized the soul of the nation. Harold Ickes referred to the national parks as "living pictures of the great past of our country." Franklin Roosevelt gave voice to this vision in a speech at Glacier National Park in 1934:

There is nothing so American as our national parks. The scenery and wild life are native and the fundamental idea behind the parks is native. It is, in brief, that the country belongs to the people; that what it is and what it is in the process of making is for the enrichment of the lives of all of us. Thus the parks stand as the outward symbol of this great human principle.[1]

This celebration of the land and the past defied a troubled present. With Government Rustic as their style, a corps of uprooted youth and a cadre of reoriented landscape architects created the forms of this symbolism.

The rustic style had, in fact, already established itself as the architectural dialect of the national parks and forests. As early as 1903, the Old Faithful Inn, a rambling assemblage of logs, shingles, and enormous dormers, made a major statement in the rustic vernacular at Yellowstone (fig. 67). Similar log-and-boulder structures abounded at Yosemite, Crater Lake, the Grand Canyon, and Glacier National Parks. Nonetheless, the structures of the 1900s through the 1920s were grand primary-use edifices such as Herb Maier's assortment of museums and lodges. The New Deal did not innovate so much as it mass-produced.

The only large building erected by the Depression forest-work forces was

67. *Old Faithful Inn, Yellowstone National Park, 1903.*

Timberline Lodge, a true Arts-and-Crafts tour de force to which Roosevelt paid personal homage upon its dedication in 1937 (fig. 1). The hand-craftsmanship lavished on that project ranged from the exterior beam ends shaped into bull, ram, and bear heads (fig. 2) to rugs hooked out of worn CCC uniforms and blankets. Timberline cost $650,000—the equivalent of $6.5 million in today's money. A few more projects like it and the emergency works program would have had a very different character. Instead of cabins, signs, benches, tables, observation towers, modest-size lodges, bridges, fences, grills, outhouses, and ranger stations all over the country, a few major projects would have provided abundant opportunity for employment, but only in a few locations.

The mass production of Government Rustic involved not only recruiting a host of landscape architects but also training them in the ways of the woods. Toward this end the National Park Service commissioned Albert H. Good, architect for the state park building program, to assemble a pattern book of appropriate designs. Easily the most influential of the many compilations to issue from the campaign in the forest and meadows, Good's 1935 *Park Structures and Facilities* became a bible of rural and wilderness design. The first edition sold out, and an expanded three-volume edition entitled *Park and Recreation Structures* appeared three years later. Sanford Hill maintains that the opus was "worn out from use in both national and state parks." The work retained its relevance even after the expiration of the CCC; although the materials became too expensive and cumbersome, the forms were still functional.

Park and Recreation Structures served as an indispensable architectural pattern book for the raft of minor oeuvres built by the CCC. Since then the guide has acquired secondary historic significance. First, Good's introduction and commentary presents a complete credo of the rustic style. Second, the illustrations, drawn almost entirely from the inventory of CCC work, testify to the quality of these projects. Another testimony comes from Norman Newton, who, describing the construction of a bathhouse on Lake Cayuga, mentioned that the half of the building executed by the CCC boys was of better quality than the part done by the "LEMs" or local experienced men who were part of every camp.[2]

The cumulative effect of long, concentrated hours in the wilds had its effect. The wilderness succeeded in taming its captive audience, as Howard Gregg, football hero and landscape architect, discovered after being specially flown into Yellowstone from the Midwest to confront a gang of enrollees from Hoboken and the Bronx. The New York natives, already subdued, did not require Gregg's extra brawn.[3] Supervisors and enrollees alike learned to proceed efficiently with their remote, unprecedented assignments. After three years Lloyd Fletcher reported from Sequoia that the construction forces there were relying more on plans and that the plans had become more reliable. Philip Elwood found that the "wastefulness of planless construction work during the early years of the emergency program" had been checked and that the NPS and the CCC were according architects and engineers "more recognition and responsibility."[4] The CCC boys, who, if they were promoted to foreman, could stay past the six-month limit (later expanded to two-years), also acquired expertise. The landscape architects contributed their technical knowledge of construction, grading, and surveying.

Until recently the landscape profession of the last thirty years has been inclined towards large-scale planning, sociology, and ecology; the literature and training of its early decades emphasized the basics. Albert Taylor edited a series in the quarterly professional journal *Landscape Construction,* in which he treated everything from garden steps to riprapping with the precision and thoroughness characteristic of the times. In his 1931 article for the series, Gilmore Clarke recommends that before commencing work on a stone wall, the landscape architect should provide a six-foot square sample of masonry as a guide for the workers.[5] Five years later a photograph showed Darcy Bonnet scrutinizing four such samples at Indian Lake State Park. True to this conscientious approach, the stone walls built by the CCC consisted of strategically planned elements. The builders attempted to approximate nature by laying stones along their horizontal axis and by varying their size. Correct proportion, scale, and mortaring were all considered critical to producing a pleasing rusticity. Albert Taylor's criticism of a stone picnic shelter in the Cibola National Forest in New Mexico conveys a sense of the professionalism involved in construction (fig. 68). He pointed out that "the masonry construction might have been slightly improved by not raking the joints to the depths shown in this photograph. More evidence of the mortar joints would produce a greater

68. *Cibola National Forest, New Mexico, picnic Shelter.*

effect of stability in this stone masonry, and the individual stones should be, so far as practical, laid upon a natural bed."[6] Thus a considerable degree of artistic rigor infused the apparent artlessness of the Depression-era furnishing of the national parks and forests.

The stern editorial critique found in *Park and Recreation Structures* also reveals the care and craft that suffused the rustic mode. In assessing the administrative building at Selkirk Shores State Park in New York, Good praises its notable log workmanship, the broad sweep of its roof, and its impressive length; but he upbraids it for "the severity of the concrete base, the trivial boulder masonry of the chimneys," and "the thinness of the covering material of the roof" (fig. 69).[7] Functional as well as aesthetic concerns caught the eye of Albert Good and his assisting committee, which included Herbert Maier, Tom Vint, and Norman Newton. The annotation beneath the illustration of a skater's shelter in the Blue Hills of Massachusetts lauds the simple form and economy of the building, but comments that a ramp would have been more suitable than stairs for the passage of skaters, and deplores the raw, unsightly cut in the slope behind the building.

The text of the guide also reveals the extent to which these park architects were willing to employ deception to further their cause. For instance, it discloses the fact that the Missionary-style refectory at Corpus Christi State Park in Texas is composed not of stone, but rather of caliche, a clay and cement mixture, simulated to look like the real thing (fig. 57). CCC-built stone bridges, culverts, and drinking fountains frequently consist of concrete with a masonry appliqué. The tremendous value placed upon achieving a naturalistic appearance inspired dextrous sleight-of-hand and prodigious feats of manual labor.

The landscape architect schooled in the construction of four-car garages

69. *Selkirk Shores State Park, New York State, Administrative Building.*

and Italianate pergolas had to adapt to the canyons and groves of the Depression. The designers had to work with an administrative dictum limiting the cost of each building to fifteen hundred dollars. They also had to consider the skills of the men they had. In his report from Sequoia for the 1937–38 season, Lloyd Fletcher recounts how these factors affected his architectural decisions. He assigned the enrollees the project of constructing an equipment shed whose unfinished interior suited their rudimentary level of skill. For the design of a fire station he opted for adobe rather than wood because the use of baked mud obviated the knowledge of framing and made efficient use of available materials.[8] For people like Fletcher, resource books like *Park and Recreation Structures* were of invaluable assistance.

Given the essentials—summed up by Sanford Hill as "good commanding and good mess"—the CCC excelled. The desertion rate overall was between one and two percent a month. Political machinations were remarkably few, although it has been suggested that foremen and technical advisors had to be good Democrats. However, compared to other New Deal creations, such as the WPA, the CCC steered a lofty course. An investigation in 1936 revealed that only twenty percent of the employees were chosen from political lists. Nor was that minority necessarily incompetent.[9]

More significant in the long run was the CCC's success in inspiring an interest in the woods. The lasting achievements of the Tree Army far outweigh the repercussions of patronage or petty wrongdoing. Beyond stone tables and fire trails, the CCC left a patrimony of men dedicated to the outdoors and skilled in appropriate trades. Many CCC youths continued on in the park and forest line of work. A regional forester for Alaska, the regional director of thirteen forests in the Northern Great Plains, the superintendent of Mount Rushmore, and at least one assistant regional director of the National Park Service counted among CCC alumni. In addition, a good many skilled plumbers, masons, electricians, and other craftsmen graduated from the ranks of the CCC.[10] Even if they didn't become master masons or regional foresters, enough CCC members valued that brief episode in their lives to honor it by creating a National Alumni Association, which boasted seven thousand members in 1981, only four years after its inception.

The applause accorded the CCC has eclipsed dissenting voices raised during its tenure. At the time, purist conservationists viewed the Corps's arrival in the nation's woods as a farmer might welcome a herd of elephants to a lettuce field. The need to keep the army of youths occupied meant that hitherto virgin territory resounded with the sound of falling trees and the spectacle of outcrops being moved to make way for fire breaks, truck roads, and recreation circulation routes. One detractor—Norman Livermore, later California Secretary of Resources under Ronald Reagan—called the CCC the number one threat to the wilderness. He decried the fact that the proportion of roads to trails had doubled in the national forests since the inception of the Civilian Conservation Corps. Robert Marshall also deplored the popularity of ridge roads. With a panoply of CCC projects encroaching, Newton Drury, investigating officer for California's State Parks and National Parks Director from 1940 to 1952, fought hard to keep the CCC out of Point Lobos.[11] To these purists, the CCC was a noxious harbinger of civilization.

The elite position enjoyed by CCC "powder monkeys," workers trained in demolition, suggests that the fears of these conservationists were not unfounded. One powder monkey boasted that "these men put their mark in many of our forty-eight states in opening up the wilderness." Other shortcomings of the CCC stemmed from inadequate Forest Service policy. Thousands of hours spent eradicating *ribes* bushes did not succeed in eliminating the blister rust disease noxious to several pine species. Sixty-five million man-days expended on fire fighting cancelled the regenerative effects of controlled burning.[12] In these cases, however, the Forest Service more than the CCC must bear the burden for unwise tactics.

Although the policies behind CCC work in the forests sometimes lacked clear direction, the bulk of the camps assigned to the Department of Agriculture spearheaded a great insurgence of silviculture. The achievements in the Sparta District in northern Wisconsin gives some idea of the Herculean labor performed. In eighteen months one camp planted 4,703 acres of land, constructed 20 miles of telephone lines, forged 44 miles of forest service truck trails, improved 512 acres of timber, and deposited 144,500 fish in the area's lakes. By 1941 the CCC claimed to have planted two billion trees, twelve for every American citizen.[13]

70. Arapahoe National Forest, Colorado, unthinned stand of trees, 1972.

The outback districts of this country still give evidence of the CCC presence. In many forests two contrasting, adjoining stands of trees indicate that one once received CCC attention. In the Arapahoe National Forest in Colorado, the trees in the stand thinned by the CCC have acquired some girth, whereas those in the neglected companion stand are scrawny and stunted (figs. 70, 71). Forest stands such as those of the Arapahoe or the Black Hills in North Dakota gained 77 percent as much growth in a few years after CCC thinning as they had in the previous 45 years.[14] Now these stands are once again in need of attention.

Indeed, across the land nature has been erasing the work of the CCC. Firebreaks have grown over; check dams have disintegrated; artificial lakes and ponds have become eutrophic. The Ponderosa Way no longer starves fires from Bakersfield to Redding in California's back country; brush and trees have reclaimed it. Miles of footpaths through the towering redwoods of the northern California coast have disappeared.[15] Acres of spilled rubble signal the site of former legions of arroya dams once ranked in mighty array at the San Bernardino and Angeles National Forests (fig. 72). The man-made lake at California's Pinnacles National Monument is expiring; pollution has preempted the Green Mountains' Hapgood Pond (fig. 73).[16] If the CCC had won its battle to become permanent, these natural encroachments might have been forestalled.

71. *Arapahoe National Forest, Colorado, thinned stand of trees, 1972.*

72. *Angeles National Forest, California, arroya dams, 1934.*

73. *Hapgood Pond, Green Mountains National Forest.*

Still, although the wilderness has regained much of its commandeered territory, outposts attesting to the New Deal occupation are common. Both the Park Service and the Forest Service revered durability, and the philosophy guiding public recreation design of the time, as explained by Darcy Bonnet, was that the public would safeguard facilities that were well built and well maintained. Bonnet's successor cites evidence that proves the wisdom of that attitude. In the 1970s the Forest Service modernized the Applewhite Campground in the San Bernardino National Forest by installing "vandal-proof" facilities—which were promptly vandalized. Not to be defeated, the Forest Service then returned to the site and restored the CCC-built structures it had previously ignored.[17]

Although Bonnet claims that many of the fabrications in the California forest have vanished, Wayne Iverson, the landscape architect who succeeded him, disagrees. Iverson extols the masonry of the thirties as the ultimate in stonework. Reports from national parks and forests across the land attest to the survival of CCC construction work. Tourists to the Monongahela National Forest in West Virginia still use "most of the recreation facilities and many of the buildings" built by twelve CCC camps. Lee Roberts, who had been a LEM (Local Experienced Man) with a company building recreation facilities in the national parks in southern Utah, returned forty years later and found to his delight that his handiwork was "still in good condition and in good use."[18] Most of the CCC veterans, returning to the fields where they labored, find that much has survived since their departure. Not only earth-hugging architecture, but such niceties as precipitous overlooks, humorous signs, and leafen play equipment continue to entice the wilderness traveler (figs. 74–76).

In 1939, enrollment in the CCC fell off, accompanied by a decline in the quality of supervision. A new attitude toward building in the rough accompanied this attrition. Critics began attacking what they saw as an overemphasis on permanence, citing a lack of flexibility that did not allow for convenient alterations in design and location.[19] The Government Rustic style was seen as false and overwrought. A landscape architect who was an inspector for Yosemite led the assault, writing, "There is nothing so quarrelsome with a friendly park as a building outruding the rudeness of the pioneer: cartoons of his dignified deprivations. These rough buildings, wrangling with nature, can already be numbered in legions."[20]

The course of development at Big Bend National Park tucked into the heel of Texas corresponds to the dissolution of the image-laden style of the 1930s. A series of preliminary sketches executed in 1939 depict the park settlement in a composite ranch and missionary style. The lodge, like the other assorted outbuildings, was to be a low, sprawling structure with a tile roof and the look of adobe (fig. 77). But none of these buildings ever materialized, as the nation turned to preparation for war. The CCC faded out, leaving the Big Bend with a motley collection of prefabricated huts (fig. 78).

This early use of prefabricated structures was a portent of things to come. The high costs of labor and materials after the war have forced the Park and

74. Chiricahua National Monument, Arizona, overlook.

75. *Bastrop State Park, Texas, sign.*

Forest Services to turn to catalogues for ready-made camping facilities, out-houses, and other small structures. Even if a project is custom-designed, the system of competitive bidding often acts to compromise the results. And even when the financial resources are available, where, as one supervisor phrased it, can you find a man who can cope a log? Even if the workers can be located, the resulting structure tends toward an unexciting countenance like that of the smooth stone wall and finely milled shingles of the cubist Mammoth Lakes

76. *A. D. Taylor surveying recreation structure, Willamette National Forest, Oregon.*

77. Big Bend National Park, Texas, study for Hacienda Lodge, 1939.

Visitors' Center in Inyo National Forest in California (fig. 79). More prosaic buildings have followed. The concrete block lodge and cafeteria built at Big Bend in the last year of Mission '66, the National Park's building campaign, are hardly "living pictures of the great past of our country" (fig. 80). The heroic myth of the pioneer had been displaced as a basis for interpreting the wilderness.

The patriotic and democratic cast of the landscape mission of the Depression years encouraged the profession of landscape architecture to realign itself. Already excited by the modern movement in art and architecture, the young rebels were chafing to smash the old idols. As a junior instructor at Yale, Christopher Tunnard defiantly proclaimed, "Gardening is not a fine art: it is an art of the people." He demanded the destruction of the accepted attitude of the garden as picture, and thus the elimination of axes, vistas, and any allusion to the romantic or the picturesque. Inspiration, he insisted, should flow not from Europe or the Colonial past, but from the vernacular images of oil derricks, dams, truck gardens, and orchards. Another Young Turk, Garrett Eckbo, voiced similar convictions which deepened when a stint with the Farm Security Administration "strongly politicized" him.[21] In effect, the Depression promoted the cause of these would-be emancipators.

While the youthful landscape architects were protesting, their senior counterparts were already drawing their keep from the newly calibrated world of the New Deal. Gilmore Clarke, who worked for the Bronx Parkway Com-

78. Big Bend National Park, Texas, the Basin.

mission, the Westchester County Park Commission, and as a consultant for Robert Moses, represented the new breed of public service landscape architect. But most landscape architects straddled both sides of the garden wall. Arthur Shurcliff, one of Boston's most prominent practitioners and a principal in the restoration of Colonial Williamsburg, was also an advisor for the development of Franconia and Crawford Notches in the White Mountains. A member of the National Capitol Park and Planning Commission, Henry Hubbard oversaw the progress of Washington's extensive activity in open space development, and he wore another hat as consultant for the TVA. The emergence of the public landscape offered Frank Waugh the opportunity to broadcast the young iconoclasts' demand for respect of the natural landscape. In fact, Waugh preached ecology to the national parks and forests long before its time. In his article "Planning of the Recreational Use of Our Wildlands," Waugh espoused low-impact design which would safeguard marginal brush and woodland. He urged the careful study of transitional zones between one landscape type and another so that these fragile sectors might be reproduced and incorporated with recreational spaces.[22] A composite profession further varied by the eclectic disposition of the age, landscape architecture was able to adapt quickly to the changed scenario.

79. *Inyo National Forest, California, Mammoth Lakes Visitors' Center, 1969.*

80. *Big Bend National Park, Texas, lodge, 1966.*

Critical to the landscape architects' success in assuming leadership of the New Deal conservation and recreation movement was the essential conservatism of the profession. The Roosevelt Adminstration sought not so much to change as to preserve or revive esteemed ideals. This was a decade that clung to water chains and rustic cabins. Because they shared the same myths, landscape architects could ally themselves with the workers, the military, and the civil service to create a cautious, homogeneous, and astonishingly congenial vision on the land.

Outside the government sphere the architectural revolution, with its self-professed freedom from conventions and formulas, was making headway. Excluding maverick Midwesterner Jens Jensen and the young rebels whose impact was still more in word than plan, architects, not landscape architects, pursued the most unconventional garden design. Richard Neutra in Los Angeles and Frank Lloyd Wright were taking their cues from the land itself rather than from any preestablished garden tradition. Toward the end of the Federal Works Program, this new empirical approach surfaced at such projects as the Woodminster Cascade and Redwood Regional Park.

The myths and symbols that had for generations covered the land did not altogether disintegrate. The landscape and buildings of the national parks and forests invoked the spirit of democracy and pioneer strength. Landscape architect and laborer alike toiled in the name of these values. Today no such unanimity could unite a national conservation and works program. The giant

81. *San Bernardino National Forest, California, bikers' wedding.*

national preserves are now seen either as the ultimate wilderness adventure, or as so inviolate and sacrosanct as almost to forbid entry. Adherents of these contemporary attitudes would regard with horror the glee with which their 1930s counterparts toted up miles of truck trails, roads, piping, and wiring. But in some instances, ideology aside, urbanization has simply encroached upon a park or forest. It is now not untypical for a rustic CCC-built campground such as the one in San Bernardino National Forest to host a bikers' wedding (fig. 81).

CHAPTER EIGHT

The Rise of Kudzu and the Spread of the Black Locust

O N A FARM that once belonged to H. E. Curtis in Magnum, Oklahoma, stands an Austrian pine well over forty feel tall. The tree itself would scarcely be noteworthy but for the fact that it is the first tree set out in a mammoth federal afforestation program that was originally expected to freckle the Great Plains with over three billion seedlings.[1] The Curtis tree, planted in March, 1935, by a WPA laborer, signaled the beginning of the Prairie States Forestry Project and of direct relations between farmers and the federal government.

The Prairie States Forestry Project and the Soil Conservation Service, along with price support, were Washington's principal wedges in its concerted advance into farming. The large-scale federal commitment to agriculture was compelled by washed-out hills, denuded plains, and exhausted bottom lands which blotched the American image of bountiful fields and towering forests. The debilitated state of the land mocked the ideals of pioneer and frontier. This vision of a virgin past that had inspired the planning for recreation and reforestation now invigorated the cause for soil conservation.

Dust roused public awareness of the deterioration of the land. Spectacular dust storms, precipitated by careless farming and a long spell of dry weather, occurred in the springs of 1934 and 1935. The dust cloud that accumulated during the 1934 storm swept out into the Atlantic, in the process blotting out the sun over large parts of the nation and sifting into New York City windows.[2] Dramatic photographs record the devastation and dislocation attendant upon the drought and dust storms. Two typical photos, taken the summer of 1936 in Bottineau, North Dakota, show the effects of both soil loss and the dislocations it caused (figs. 82, 83). The desperate victims, so-called

82. *Bottineau area, North Dakota. Abandoned farm, 1936.*

"Okies," exited en masse, leaving behind wastelands like the plains of central South Dakota, where crop yields were so low that as late as 1937 they weren't worth harvesting. The Dust Bowl was the ecological equivalent of the collapse of the stock market, and its reverberations were felt across the country. As "Black Thursday" came to connote financial disaster, so the phrase "the dirty thirties" described the distress of the land, in particular the fragility of the topsoil. Government action followed upon public awareness. Prior to the first big dust storm in 1934, the PWA had subsidized an intensive erosion survey, which concluded that half the nation was suffering from moderate to severe erosion.[3] Furthermore, 14 percent of the erosion was extremely ruinous. On the basis of these disturbing findings the Soil Conservation Service emerged as a full-fledged unit of the Department of Agriculture, and the battle against erosion commenced.

The New Deal tackled the erosion menace in three ways. First, the 1934 Taylor Grazing Act prohibited further homesteading by dedicating all remaining eligible land to controlled grazing. Second, the government pulled out of agricultural production 11.3 million substandard acres, a small fraction of which became Recreation Demonstration Areas.[4] Finally, the Roosevelt administration, in one of its characteristic romantic quirks, began in 1934 a transcontinental wind break which was known as the Prairie States Forestry Project. This massive shelterbelt inaugurated by the planting of H. E. Curtis's tree was intended to stretch from just north of Abilene, Texas to the Canadian border (fig. 84).[5] In the popular mind it has been seen as an arboreal Great

83. *Bottineau area, North Dakota. Soil erosion, 1936.*

Wall keeping out a barbarian horde of dust. In fact, the Shelterbelt was a buckshot approach to the problem of anchoring the soil to the back of the prairie. Invincible or not, the sheer outlandish audacity of this rampart of trees evidences the urgency the era attached to the soil erosion issue. The big, brash solution also reflects an American penchant for dramatic action that shows up in many Depression-era land projects.

The Shelterbelt did not in fact resemble a wall. Situated in the area of transition between the tall grass prairie and short grass plains, it faced a hostile soil and an ungracious climate. To accommodate the inhospitable terrain, the Prairie States Forestry Project tried four different types of planting: farmstead planting of six to twelve rows of trees and shrubs around farm buildings; woodland plantings for fuel, posts, poles, and game cover; solid block planting in relatively large areas of public land, and, most common, farm strips consisting of ten rows of trees spaced about ten feet apart. Most of the belts ended up in an east-west rather than north-south orientation.[6]

A tremendous research effort helped determine the most effective composition of the shelterbelts. The Forest Service's Lake States Forest Experiment Station at St. Paul, Minnesota carried out the background work. In 1935 the Lake States Station published *Possibilities of Shelterbelt Planting in the Plains Region.* This comprehensive, two-hundred-page technical source book for the Prairie States Project has been cited as a remarkable example of applied ecology.[7] As with much of the survey work done during this era, it was accomplished through the superhuman effort of a few people. In this instance three groups,

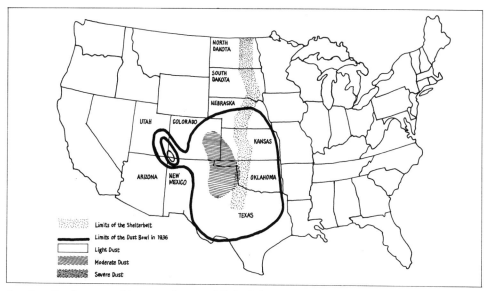

84. Dust Bowl region and location of proposed Shelterbelt.

each with an automobile, took two months to survey ten thousand plots or groups of trees in an area extending from Canada to Lubbock, Texas. The resulting report became the basis for silviculture in the Great Plains.

The ideal shelterbelt had the profile of a broad hip roof. It simulated a forest stand with a center group of fast-growing trees, surrounded by slower-growing evergreens and hardwoods which finally tapered into rows of shrubs. This arrangement was expected to encourage moisture-preserving forest litter, to destroy weeds and other competitive growth, and to trap snow, which both protected the plant and animal life and acted as a water source.

A prototypical stand was planted in 1935, three miles south of Mitchell, South Dakota (fig. 85). Green ash, American elm, and Chinese elm were flanked by rows of caranga and Russian olive; two rows of cottonwood formed the center. In two years' time (when the photograph was taken) the Chinese elms and the cottonwoods were already ten feet high.

As healthy and eager as the Mitchell stand appeared after two years, chances are good that it ultimately failed. Its composition demonstrates four errors committed by the Prairie States Forestry Project. One was the mistake of planting the American elm. The dependence on the rangy cottonwood proved even more disastrous, since it proved just as vulnerable to disease. A water-loving tree, it was planted in arid areas where it became weak and susceptible to cytosper canker. Third, the Chinese elm also had a poor survival rate, and where it did thrive, it became a pest. Finally, the sample South Dakota shelterbelt may well have been improperly oriented to the prevailing wind. This turned out to be the case with many of the belts.[8] (Subsequent research

85. Prairie States Forestry Project, Mitchell, South Dakota, typical stand.

also determined that the 132-foot width of the windbreak was overenthusiastic; a 50-foot width would have sufficed.) With limited afforestation experience and only a hasty survey as preludes, the Shelterbelt was indeed a giant gamble.

Nevertheless, despite the many flaws of the Forestry Project, the individual shelterbelts that survived did accomplish their purpose. These tree barriers offered gifts of shade and beauty, reduced the problem of dust, and protected from cold. A study by the Forestry Service demonstrated that if a 30-mile-per-hour wind encounters a belt 35 feet high, the phalanx of trees diminishes the velocity of the wind to 10 miles per hour for the first 100 feet and 15 miles per hour for the next 100 feet. Generally the protected zone extends to 20 times the height of the trees, and it is possible to cut the wind in half for a considerable distance (fig. 86). A study in 1962 of 286 fields near 1930s shelterbelts confirmed that the natural blockade increased moisture retention by the soil. The protected fields had greater yields than did a test group of exposed fields.[9]

The Shelterbelt project became the fulcrum of a great deal of activity in the botanical and silvicultural worlds. The Soil Conservation stations and laboratories at Park River and Bottineau, North Dakota; Lincoln, Nebraska; and Pullman, Washington became centers for information. The demand for seeds and tree cuttings generated businesses and jobs. Beginning in the summer of 1934, many CCC camps were assigned to the Soil Conservation Service to carry out the leg work. (A caption on one National Archives photo, which

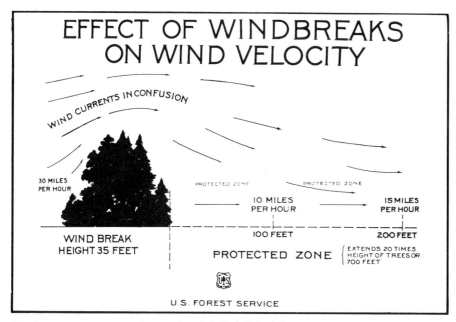

EFFECT OF WINDBREAKS
ON WIND VELOCITY

WIND CURRENTS IN CONFUSION

30 MILES
PER HOUR

PROTECTED ZONE   PROTECTED ZONE

10 MILES
PER HOUR

15 MILES
PER HOUR

100 FEET   200 FEET

WIND BREAK
HEIGHT 35 FEET

PROTECTED ZONE   EXTENDS 20 TIMES
HEIGHT OF TREES OR
700 FEET

U.S. FOREST SERVICE

86. Government promotional material on behalf of Shelterbelt.

shows CCC boys collecting willow wildings along the Missouri, notes that the
record was held by three boys who amassed twelve thousand cuttings in three
hours.) At the outset of the project, the demand for the black locust, the most
widely planted species of tree, was such that it was necessary to import seed
from abroad even though the tree is native to the North American continent.
Subsequently, a seed industry developed in Idaho, eastern Oregon, and Washington which could easily handle an order for one hundred thousand pounds of
black locust seeds.[10]

This horticultural activity also generated numerous technical breakthroughs. William Droze enumerates several, among them the production of
cottonwood seedlings from seed, the use of root pruning to achieve a critical
balance between the top and bottom of the tree, and the introduction of
refrigeration to preserve conifer stock during the transfer from nursery to
planting sites. Technological advances included the development of a special
shovel adapted for the plains and a machine which, operated by three people,
could plant up to eight thousand trees a day. This device was used into the
sixties.[11]

Measured against the expectations it generated, the Prairie States Forestry Project was only a qualified success. Funding was never adequate. In
1936, Congress refused to continue supporting the project, and it stumbled
along with alternative funding, first with money dispersed by the WPA
and then, in 1942, under the aegis of the burgeoning Soil Conservation Service. Subsumed to the purposes of this agency, arboriculture on the Great

Plains gradually became a minor addendum in the daily routine of the regional Conservation District offices.

Recent developments have hastened the decline of the Shelterbelt to little more than a historical footnote. Planted with a life expectancy of thirty to sixty years, many of the shelterbelts are expiring. Farmers are purposely destroying other stands, either to create more cropland or because the trees obstruct their roving irrigation systems. Modern government policies ignore tree-planting.

In 1956, after another bout with dust, Washington launched a twenty-five-year land reformation program in the plains. The two stated goals of this conservation effort were to convert over five million acres unsuitable as cropland to more appropriate employ as pasture, and to reseed badly depleted rangeland. Trees did not figure at all. Clearly the formulators of the Great Plains Conservation Program had assessed the results of the Prairie States Forestry Project and found it lacking. In fact, only two years before the Conservation Program began, a survey of the Depression shelterbelts revealed that only 42 percent were in good condition; 8 percent had been destroyed, 19 percent were in disrepair, and 31 percent were only in fair condition.[12]

Ironically, the 1956 effort against soil erosion and depletion hearkened back to a plan presented in opposition to the Shelterbelt in 1934. Ellsworth Huntington, a research associate in geography at Yale, recommended that the western half of the states ranging from North Dakota to the Texas panhandle should be developed for a grazing economy. Huntington deplored the implementation of expensive and exotic remedies like the arboreal American Great Wall. Donald Worster echoed Huntington in 1979 when he stated that the Shelterbelt encouraged the use of the plains for field crops, an activity for which they were unfit.

So far the results of the Great Plains Conservation Program have not supported the superiority of this approach, although the method of implementation rather than the aim may be the problem. Like its predecessor, the project was both voluntary and vastly underfunded. If, as Huntington indicated, the Shelterbelt was costly and quixotic in relation to its practical benefits, it would not be so unlike many of the New Deal undertakings. And, like the Timberline Lodge, elephantine stone outhouses, and monumental picnic furnishings, the Shelterbelt, a congenial and nostalgic interruption of the vast spaces of the prairie, has been a singular amenity of inestimable value.

The submergence of the Shelterbelt into the Soil Conservation Service added to that agency's strength. The Soil Conservation Service crusaded energetically for sound agricultural practices. With the help of CCC labor—as many as five hundred camps in 1936—the farming reform movement quickly gained momentum. Initially the Soil Conservation Service relied upon the written word and practical demonstration to spread its manifold message. It recruited farmers who were willing to build terraces, to plant according to the contours of the land, to restrict steep terrain pasture or woodlots, and to consider strip-cropping, alternating bands of clean-tilled crops, such as corn and beans, with thick-growing ones, such as hay and alfalfa. The farms employing such stratagems became models of judicious agriculture. The Conservation Service also recruited whole watersheds to demonstrate the benefits of sound farming methods. It selected demonstration farms and positioned CCC camps nearby for help in implementing erosion-prevention practices. Overall 175 such watershed demonstration areas came into being. [13] By 1937 California had three; the Ohio Valley, extending from Michigan to Tennessee, boasted fourteen.

The township of La Crosse in southwestern Wisconsin hosted a particularly intensive and well-documented watershed program. The noted naturalist Aldo Leopold acted as an unofficial monitor of this area—the Coon Creek valley. Overgrazing by cows had left the land defenseless before the flood waters of the Mississippi. [14] In a concentrated restorative effort, the Soil Conservation Service recruited 413 farms amenable to conservation precautions. They replanted woodland above a 40 percent grade, employed terracing and strip-cropping, built check dams in washed-out gullies, and planted both creek banks and gullies. From 1934 to 1942 the government monitored the earnings and production of thirty to fifty of the farms. Over these years income averaged 25 percent greater than the first year, even though crop values remained fairly constant. Coon Valley turned from despoliation to bounty.

This success depended upon cooperative acceptance of soil conservation tactics. Before the intervention of the Soil Conservation Service, the farmers of Coon Creek practiced a tentative form of erosion control by means of close-crop coverage on 10 percent or less of the land. Three years later, in 1936, 40 percent of the land received some kind of protective plant coverage, and other soil conservation tactics had radically expanded. Terracing had increased 15 percent and contour planting, formerly used on less than half of the clean-tilled crop acreage, had become almost standard. The Soil Conservation Service had transformed the La Crosse area into a paragon of ecological virtue. [15]

The government promoted soil conservation with publications which graphically dramatized its economic benefits (fig. 87). In 1937 the Conservation Service, like the Park Service, was regionalized. This move helped the fight against slipshod agriculture and facilitated the effort to douse a million of the hundred million acres in the Southeast Conservation District with the tough roots and large, shiny green leaves of the Japanese kudzu vine. [16] Before the government gave kudzu its new role it was known as "porch vine," a vigorous and effective plant for shade or ornamental use. Nevertheless, farmers feared it would become a pest, and in this case native suspicion proved justified. The seventy-three million seedlings the Soil Conservation Service planted from 1935 to 1941 formed the beachhead of a vegetative invasion that

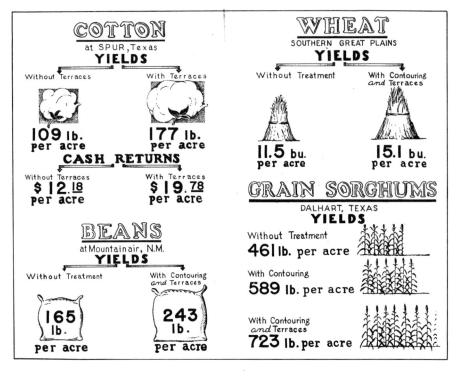

87. *Effects of contouring and terracing on crop production.*

has since subdued large areas of the South. With growth rates of up to a foot in twenty-four hours and roots that burrow down as deep as seven feet, kudzu has consolidated its hold.

Kudzu anchored soil to the land, filled the gullies, covered the denuded hills, and even fed the cattle. It also engulfed telephone poles, trees, houses, and pasture. Even its most ardent enemies credit its efficient, if overzealous, performance of its duty. A county extension agent in Georgia conceded that the controversial vine "probably saved the state from washing into the ocean."[17] Meanwhile, other critics optimistically try to devise beneficial uses for the large-leafed vine that now masks much of the South. So far schemes to make food and fuel out of the omnipresent plant have not been successful. Kudzu persists as one of the more blatant indiscretions of the thirties land revitalization effort. In direct contrast to the limited growth performance of the Shelterbelt, the kudzu vine proved itself all too dynamic.

Neither kudzu nor the shelterbelts have eradicated the erosion problem in the United States. Even a minor drought on the plains causes the dust storms to rise again. Today the rate of erosion surpasses 1930 levels. Bob Bergland, Secretary of Agriculture under Carter, "has estimated that more than fifteen million tons of topsoil flow out of the Mississippi every minute," continuing a trend evident in the thirties when eroded soil buried houses in the

Delta up to their eaves.[18] In 1934 the Soil Reconnaissance Survey estimated that half the country's land was suffering from moderate to severe erosion. A 1977 study indicated that one third of all land in the United States was experiencing excessive erosion.

Recent counteroffensives against the blight of soil loss have not been effective. For one thing, the public has been largely apathetic about the problem. Pressed by a narrowing margin between costs and profits, farmers have fallen back into methods which exacerbate the problem. Moreover, government agricultural policies have been at crosspurposes. A 1973 federal review of the Great Plains Conservation Program underscored the contradictory nature of Washington's involvement in Western farming.[19] At the same time that the USDA's crop subsidy program, which dates back to the thirties, pays farmers to grow certain crops, the soil conservation sector of the same agency is encouraging, also with monetary incentive, farmers to convert to pasture land unsuitable for crop-growing. While this contradictory and confusing barrage continues, valuable soil creeps away.

Frustrated by this crippling of the soil conservation cause, concerned agricultural observers talk of discarding the voluntary bias of federal agricultural programs. Proponents of what is called cross-compliance urge that farmers receive benefits only in return for strict observation of conservation methods. In his critique of Southern Plains agriculture, Donald Worster advocates socialist control of farms. But whether cross-compliance or socialist restraints are adopted, a resurgence of massive planting on the order of either kudzu or the Shelterbelt is unlikely. Kudzu in the South and black locust on the plains will continue to embody the Depression as poignantly and uniquely as do rough-hewn wood and rock structures in the country and rose gardens in the city.

Rearranging People on the Land: Cumberland Homesteads, Greendale, and Linelle Camp

RTHUR SCHLESINGER writes of the twenties and early thirties, "A malaise was seizing many Americans, a sense at once depressing and exhilarating, that capitalism itself was finished."[1] As the restoration of Colonial Williamsburg and the frontier artifice in the state and national parks has shown, this unease expressed itself partly in the urge to resurrect old orders. Conversely, the same disaffection surfaced in a move towards new alternative lifestyles. In this country and elsewhere people sought to fashion new societies which would allow greater mass participation. In Russia, Germany, and Italy this communitarian reform spirit was perverted. In England, the rise of the collective will manifested itself constructively in government regulation and planning for urban growth. The concept of controlled growth spread to Scandinavia and migrated to the United States, where Roosevelt's "Brain Trust" was zealously trying to introduce a socialist esprit to a land where every man still fiercely guarded his castle. Cumberland Homesteads, Greendale, and Linelle Camp arose from this struggle. The results were, as might be expected, fragmentary. Nevertheless, these three communities and their cohorts have persisted. Of their original bias toward a collective ideal, only faint echoes are heard, but the boldness of Washington's only frankly ideological venture into new town planning has inspired three generations of planners.

Although American intellectuals were enthralled by the credo of communism, the agricultural population was obdurate or indifferent. Nonetheless, a back-to-the-land movement that had been gaining momentum since the turn of the century paved the way for experiments in cooperative living. Religious organizations such as the Jewish Agricultural Society, quixotic individuals like the prominent New York agrarian Ralph Borsodi, and even the state of California had been involved in launching communitarian rural settlements.[2] An ongoing lobbying effort sought to draw the federal government into rural resettlement. Finally some people within the New Deal, especially Eleanor Roosevelt and Rexford Tugwell, seized upon the colonization phenomenon as the ideal testing ground for various reforms.

Planning utopian communities has been both a much-honored and a much-maligned occupation. The Roosevelt administration plunged boldly into resettlement, securing loans for private housing, subsidizing low-income housing, and ultimately planning and building whole new communities. So convoluted was the housing bureaucracy that a diagram is necessary to parse it (chart 4). Three settlements drawn from this chart—Cumberland Homesteads in Tennessee, Greendale in Wisconsin, and the Linelle Camp in Tulare County, California—impart a sense of the broad range of the New Deal effort, both in what was attempted and what was achieved.

When Eleanor Roosevelt surveyed the progress at Cumberland Homesteads in July, 1934 from the back of Paul Monday's lumber truck, a sizeable portion of the undulating wooded tract of twenty thousand acres had been cleared. Some fields of crops were even producing. The homesteaders, dislocated miners, some unemployed lumbermen, and a few poor farmers, camped in their barns while they worked on their houses. About 12 of the 253 total homesteads had been completed, along with almost 54 barns and 41 poultry houses.[3] Eleanor Roosevelt noted that progress had been made, contrary to widespread skepticism. The community already displayed the well-ordered and attractive look it bears to this day (fig. 88). Stone houses were set back 75 to 100 feet on lots of about 16 acres with 40-foot frontages (fig. 89). The masonry construction, the regularity, and the spaciousness of both the land and the two-story dwellings distinguished this community from the surrounding locale, with its modest one-story wood-frame houses set at random upon the rolling landscape.

The settled, placid outward appearance of Cumberland belied the reality inside. All the homesteads experienced protracted difficulties and frequent dissension. Economic maladies also afflicted the four experimental "stranded industrial workers'" communities, of which Cumberland was one.[4] The government's revolving set of rules and fluctuating credo only exacerbated the confusion.

The deficiencies were architectural as well as economic and administrative. The Cumberland houses proved to be veritable ice boxes. One fireplace and a stove were totally inadequate to the task of heating the oversized homes, most of which lacked cellars. The project architect from Pennsylvania had not known how cold it got 1,850 feet up on the Cumberland Plateau. Nevertheless, Cumberland's problems paled before those of Eleanor's pet project, Arthurdale, where one mix-up after another—like the procure-

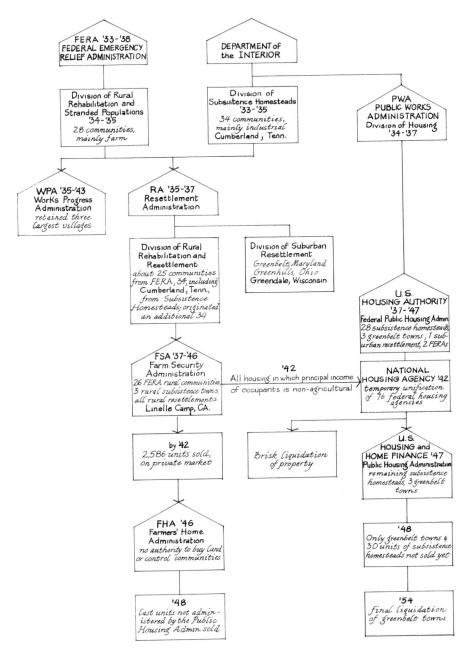

New Deal Ventures in Housing[1]

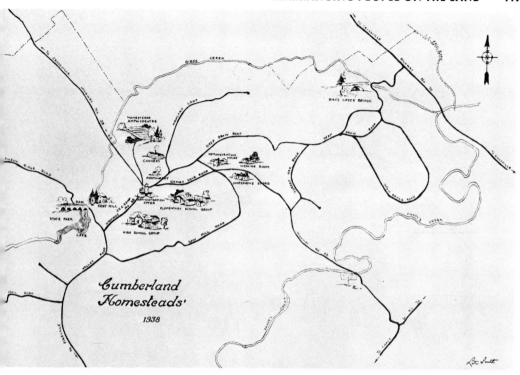

88. *Cumberland Homesteads, Tennessee, plan, 1938.*

ment of fifty-one useless prefabricated houses—made the project a national laughing stock. Less ambitious and consequently less vulnerable, the urban homesteads easily keyed into an existing and proximate economy. However, the lack of problems and strife attending the metropolitan projects, such as Longview Homesteads in Washington or Dalworthington Gardens in Arlington, Texas, makes them intrinsically less interesting than Cumberland or Arthurdale.

The greenbelt towns have historically enjoyed more repute, because they were physically more daring, but of all the colonization schemes, the rural resettlement towns provided the most complete laboratory for New Deal social and economic theory. The loftiness and multiplicity of the resettlement program's aims are apparent in the optimistic descriptive statement offered by John Nolen, a preeminent city planner and consultant to the project: "The subsistence homestead is a combination of several things which are usually separate, for example, industry and gardening or farming; part-time industrial employment and desirable provision for food and shelter; work and better use of leisure time; decentralization and new recentralization."[5] Because of their remote locations, the communities had to combine farming and industry. In the greenbelt towns the inhabitants could, when businesses were not at once forthcoming, commute to the nearby population centers. Moreover, the tradi-

89. Cumberland Homesteads, Tennessee, house.

tion in areas like the Cumberland Plateau was already one of subsistence farming. To this tradition the New Deal offered some new and intriguing angles.

The government's attempts to bring economic diversity to Eastern Tennessee were mostly hit-and-miss. The homesteaders started out with a communal flock of eight thousand federally provided barred Plymouth Rock pullets. Later it added a cooperative cannery, a sorghum plant, and a hosiery mill. The farms, only fifteen or twenty acres each, were too small to make a profit; the sorghum plant and cannery failed. Of five hosiery mills at various homestead communities, only the one at Cumberland managed to turn a small profit.

Despite these dreary statistics Cumberland not only survived, but in many ways thrived. Nor was it the only survivor. By 1942 only 18 percent of the population of the homesteads still retained by the Farm Security Administration had departed.[6] In succeeding years Cumberland even lured additional

90. Cumberland Homesteads, Tennessee, Homestead School.

businesses, so that today it boasts a couple of textile factories and, on the same property that once held the cannery and sorghum mill, a rubber products plant.

The real center of life at Cumberland was never the sorghum mill or the hosiery plant. Industry only propped up an enriched life of field and factory, arts and crafts, and social and political involvement. Here as elsewhere in the New Deal the quality-of-leisure theme surfaced boldly. Education was key to this new life. Long after all physical traces of the initial industrial endeavors had vanished, the prepossessing Homestead School still anchors the town. A rambling chain of shed-roofed stone buildings, it defines one edge of the village green (fig. 90). This school not only educated the children, but also tutored the adults in an array of subjects ranging from cooking to blueprint reading. A demonstration house, a weaving room, and the unavoidable New Deal outdoor amphitheater once complemented the school activities. A flotilla of arts and crafts instructors, home economists, agronomists, and social workers descended upon this Brave New World.[7] Indeed, the frenzy of instruction that occurred in these stranded workers' towns presaged the contemporary enthusiasm for adult education.

Farming and homemaking in particular were stressed. In the finest tradition of thirties didacticism, a press release by the Division of Subsistence Homesteads announced the credo behind this emphasis: "The central idea underlying the development of the Cumberland project is not only to provide homes for the homesteaders but to retrain them for self-support, and emphasize the fact that leisure time should and can be used to provide the things which a

man and his family need."[8] In line with this approach Cumberland Homesteads became the base for at least five agricultural studies. "Home Production
of Food Supplies" regulated the diets of twenty-three families by, among other
means, introducing them to soybeans and challenging them to minimize their
grocery bill. Caught in the spirit of frugality, one family whittled their annual
food bill down from $29.95 to $9.91. Other tracts investigated methods for
potato-growing, the cultivation of strawberries, the raising of goats, and land
clearance.[9] But agriculture did not go on to play a major role in the settlement
of Cumberland. Only some home gardens, a few livestock, and some leased-
out bean fields remain from the early self-subsistence days. On the other hand,
agriculture in the area, animated by a sudden abundance of cheap TVA
fertilizer, did profit from these pioneering research studies.

The New Deal legacy is writ by more than beans and potatoes. Cumberland, or Homestead, as it is now called, has evolved from an experimental
colony to "a sort of high-class suburb." The amphitheater, weaving, and
demonstration buildings have disappeared, but on the walls of one home hang
beguiling hooked rugs depicting local scenes, and painted studies of native
flora. The artist is Amy Cox Harshman, who was an original settler of Cumberland. She says that the art classes she took "made everything in the world
looked different."[10]

Like many of the New Deal land experiments, Homestead embodies and
symbolizes sacred precepts of American culture. In its case what it symbolizes,
but not the force of the symbolism, has changed. In 1971 a young entrepreneur
named Miles Clark chose Homestead as the site for a general store which
earned a national reputation catering to the back-to-the-land movement that
spanned the sixties and seventies. Appalachia drew Miles Clark, as it drew the
Subsistence Homesteads administration and other outlanders, because of its
mythic quality. Appalachia represents to America age-old, rural self-sufficiency. It is an area where, until recently, people still lived in centuries-old
patterns. The Blue Ridge Parkway and the homestead towns of Arthurdale and
Tygert Valley in West Virginia, Westmoreland in Pennsylvania, and Cumberland in Tennessee reify the Depression-era fascination with backwoods
mountain existence. In the sixties, the concentration of social welfare programs in this area—Appalachian Volunteer, VISTA, and the Community
Action Program among others—expressed not only the area's economic need
but also its potent allure. The myth was still active when Miles Clark arrived in
the early seventies and opened his store. The Cumberland Homestead not
only embodied the legend, but embodied it with unusual grace and harmony.

Miles Clark's Cumberland General Store does not reflect life as lived in
modern Homestead. Likewise the New Deal's vision did not address the reality
of Southern Mountain existence. The New Deal used the myth of idealized,
agrarian Appalachia for sociopolitical ends. Cumberland, like the athletic
fields, the playgrounds, and the group camps, was another venture in Washington's line of community experiments. In contrast, the back-to-the land

movement of the sixties and seventies, like the current fitness fad, has been private and experiential, a testing of the self rather than society. Cumberland General Store provides the implements—crosscut saws and canning jars—for this challenge. The residents of Homestead pass the store on their way to the Kroger's in Crossville. No government policy involves them in the latter-day back-to-the-land experience. The American dream for Homestead's residents—Depression or contemporary—cleaves close to the creature comforts of modern society, a safe distance from the wearisome lot that was the true Appalachia. Neither New Deal or New Age agrarianism has been able to deflect the Southern Mountain momentum towards life in the consumer mainstream.

The Roosevelt administration was not always unified about the ideology behind its return-to-the-land policies. In 1935, in a typical New Deal shuffle, the Resettlement Administration subsumed the Division of Subsistence Homesteads, along with the philosophy of a dual agricultural and industrial career championed by Roosevelt and agricultural economist M. L. Wilson, head of the division. Rexford Tugwell, former professor of economics at Columbia and the division's controversial new administrator, dismissed both the two-strand concept and remote locales in favor of suburban development accessible to city job markets.[11]

The greenbelt towns, although concerned with the cooperative ideal and the integration of farming and industry, took a less radical path towards a new society. But they were more ambitious technically than the subsistence settlements. No longer would a Pennsylvania architect adapt his state's vernacular to Tennessee based on ignorance of high country weather. The formation of the Resettlement Administration signaled a turn toward high-visibility, state-of-the-art architecture and planning. The questions of road length and greenbelt width now superceded the questions of chicken breed or tool selection. The suburban town program collected many famous designers. Beginning with Henry Wright and Clarence Stein, the creators of the innovative suburb of Radburn, the consultant staff starred Tracy Augur, Earle Draper, and Catherine Bauer, while active personnel included Roland Wank, Albert Mayer, Hale Walker, Elbert Peets, and Jacob Crane. All of these people were involved with wider New Deal building and planning.

Despite these impressive names, the greenbelt towns have not survived nearly as intact as has small, remote Cumberland. Greenbelt outside Washington and Greenhills in the vicinity of Cincinnati have succumbed to urban sprawl and freeway squeeze. The half-mile-wide greenbelts that were to protect these communities have dwindled under the onslaught of development, which has been less than sympathetic to their purpose. At both locations a chaotic mass of roads and regimented housing overwhelm the carefully developed schema of winding paths, cul-de-sacs, superblocks and other devices adopted to tame the internal combustion engine and to foster harmony and joy.

In recent years, 3,500-acre Greendale has been the most discussed of the three completed communities because it retains more of its original character, subsequent development having been more accommodating (figs. 91, 92). Moreover, its Colonial-style wood-frame and concrete block construction, its greater reliance upon single-family housing, and its use of picturesque "green-ways" combined to create a more appealing image than the severe *moderne* and plain row-house construction of the other two developments. The current acclaim of Greendale demonstrates a shift in taste. Originally interest focused on Greenbelt, the most faithful adherent to the streamlined look in building, the only true disciple of the Radburn superblock, and the most accessible subject for the New York–centered world of architectural and social critics.

Taken together these towns were, as Lewis Mumford noted in 1938, incomplete demonstrations of avant-garde city planning principles, but they did not, as some recent criticism would have it, create "scarcely a ripple of effect on the country's thought and outlook."[12] The greenbelt towns drew upon England's garden city tradition as well as a long line of native developments reaching back to Colonial Williamsburg and extending, in the twentieth century, to Radburn, New Jersey.

Washington's radical departure into the business of social planning and innovative urban design generated enough controversy to imprint these three communities on the American mind. The Resettlement Administration may have failed to make the amenities of advanced town planning available to the

91. *Greendale, Wisconsin, plan, 1930s.*

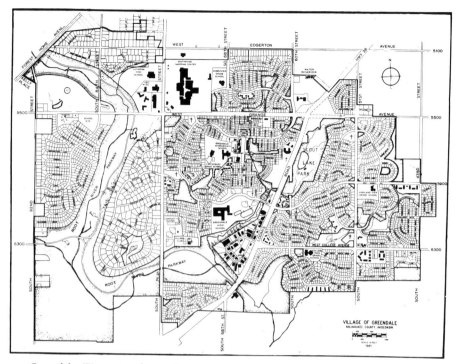

92. Greendale, Wisconsin, plan, 1981.

poor, but it did not fall short of its goal to produce national models of city design.

Although recent planning literature has accorded little consideration to the greenbelt towns, numerous examples of their resilient influence can be found from the fifties and sixties. One of the most influential books was Clarence Stein's *Toward New Towns for America,* which gives ample play to Greenbelt and meritorious notice to its partners. This volume, which covers only six other housing schemes, all from the twenties and thirties, continues to be an indispensable part of architecture and planning students' education. The greenbelt communities have also affected federal housing policy. When the new Housing and Urban Development Department was tooling up for Washington's reentry into community-building in the mid-sixties, it hired Albert Mayer, architect of Greenbrook, the fourth and unrealized greenbelt town, to reassess the New Deal developments. One of Mayer's conclusions—that private investment alone could not provide low-cost housing—reinforced the government's intention, carried out the next year, to establish a revolving fund to assist the creation of new communities that offered housing for those of modest means.

Architectural critics look for evidence of success or failure in three-dimensional form, not in government policy or student reading assignments.

Here the effect of the greenbelt towns is less directly demonstrable. Although greenbelts did not become an integral part of succeeding developments, the related concept of large areas of communal open space did—especially in townhouse developments. Often casting this open space in the form of a golf course created a primary attraction as well as a source of revenue. Limiting the mobility of the automobile has also become commonplace in towns and subdivisions from Washington to Los Angeles. And anyone who has ever been lost in Columbia, Maryland, Reston, Virginia, or countless other developments across the nation knows only too well the omnipresence of the cul-de-sac in postwar new towns. Though there may be no duplicate of Greendale, with its pleasing homes, shaded walks, harmonious commercial center, and rim-running woodland, its image and those of the other two greenbelt cities have been approximated all over the country from Jonathan, Minnesota to Foster City, California.

None of these three New Deal communities managed to live up to the self-sufficient, communal heights of glory anticipated by their planners. The subsequent history of the highly favored Cumberland, when compared with the progress of Greendale, in part justifies the time and expense devoted to the Tennessee settlement. By 1958, when Greendale finally secured its first industry, Homestead already had a shirt factory, a sweater factory, a nylon lace plant, a yardstick factory, a saw mill, and several rock quarries.[13] As further proof of its prosperity, Cumberland augmented its original grocery store with two more small markets and a trading post of regional import. A town planned to be three times the size of Homestead, Greendale made an ambitious debut with six cooperative stores, a consumer-owned movie theater, tavern, and gasoline station. These cooperative ventures did not last through the forties.[14] With regional shopping centers springing up around it, commercial enterprise in Greendale has dwindled to convenience stores, more on a line with the humbler Homestead.

Agriculture, as mentioned, was also intended to be a vital component of the suburban resettlement towns, although naturally less critical in the greenbelt towns than in the Subsistence Homesteads. While Cumberland had its eight thousand Plymouth red pullets, Greendale sported two herds of cattle and two pasteurization plants. Plans for a collective farm in the greenbelt did not materialize, but several preexisting farms were remodeled and leased back to operators.[15] However, the farmers tended to bypass Greendale for the more consequential markets of Milwaukee. Allotment gardens, laid out and actively cultivated for some years in all three communities, supported the strong subsistence theme that played through all the Roosevelt resettlement schemes. Now, as a village that has evolved from 572 housing units to a city of some 16,000 people, Greendale has lost almost all trace of its agrarian past.

Despite the smothering process of urbanization, the New Deal towns' jaunty two-story white frame houses with screened porches and kitchens facing leafy cul-de-sacs still transmit a sense of the original idealism that produced Greendale and its cohorts (fig. 93). Some inhabitants are still holdovers from the town's formative years, although not as many as at Cumberland, where approximately half of the population has remained. By 1942, Greendale lost only 9 percent of its population and six years later 54 percent still held on, a feat of some note in view of the fact that the government refused to give up control of its suburban progeny until 1952, when the tenants were finally able to buy their own homes.[16] (In contrast, the Cumberland homesteaders entered into negotiations to buy their houses as early as 1939.) This tenant loyalty in face of much frustration indicated the Resettlement Administration's success in creating livable environments, even if it failed to implement some of its communitarian ideals. In fact, one satisfied resident of Greenbelt was Rexford Tugwell himself.

More Cumberland residents would have been content to stay in their government-built town, but could not afford to buy their homes. Almost invariably the New Deal consciously selected against the needy in creating attractive, innovative shelter in order to maximize the potential for the success of their experiments. Greendale was so far out of reach of the poor that the base income of its residents exceeded the salary of half of the factory workers in the Milwaukee area. The average income of a Greendale resident in 1936 was $1,624; the government-designated poverty line was $1,000.[17] New towns

93. *Greendale, Wisconsin, cul-de-sac, 1972.*

were not the solution, as Albert Mayer was later to realize, for housing the poor.

Nonetheless, when confronted with the housing crisis presented by a roaming horde of up to half a million migrant farm workers, the federal architects and planners of the Depression did prove themselves capable of supplying housing at a rock-bottom price that did not altogether forego the ideals of the subsistence and greenbelt communities. The government built a motley collection of aluminum shelters, barracks-like row houses, and tiny cottages which, although a far cry from the sturdy stone houses or neat, white wooden homes of Cumberland and Greendale, in their disposition and development nevertheless exerted an influence far beyond what might be expected.

In order to cope with the homeless farm laborers, the Resettlement Administration, which had once been the Division of Subsistence Homesteads, became in turn the Farm Security Administration. This was a high-intensity operation that, in addition to managing the greenbelt towns and subsistence communities inherited from its predecessor agencies, by 1942 had churned out thirty mobile camps and forty-two permanent camps to accommodate the nomadic farm population.[18] The migrant labor aspect of the operation was largely confined to the West Coast. There, untrammeled by visions of Pennsylvania Dutch dwellings or Williamsburg restorations—which respectively inspired Cumberland and Greendale—the young West Coast architects drew upon both the European avant-garde and indigenous culture to create communities that might feature adobe housing with a hint of Corbusier or a park with random, staccato lines of trees redolent of the strokes of Miro or Kandinsky. The resulting work—programmatic and au courant—received unqualified praise from architectural critic Talbot Hamlin, who cited it as "a lesson for everyday architecture," because "new and beautiful architectural forms" had been derived from an economical, no-nonsense approach.[19]

The politicians and journalists who lambasted with some justification the excesses of the greenbelt and subsistence communities would have been hard put to accuse the migrant labor camps of being lavish. So essential was the need they filled and so minimal their manner of complying that these colonies, perhaps alone among the New Deal settlements, have not appreciated in value, even where the problem of transiency has disappeared. Unlike Arthurdale, where university professors jostle for space once occupied by ex-miners, or Cumberland, termed by one resident "the better end of Crossville," gentrification has not touched the migrant labor camps.[20]

A visit to the Linelle Camp outside Farmersville in central California confirms the impression that the camp's basic function of providing housing for the agrarian poor has not radically altered, although its occupants are no longer migrants. (About 5 of the total 168 families are descendants of the original Okie influx.[21]) The inhabitants are now overwhelmingly Mexican or Mexican-American, and many seem to be on disability or other forms of government aid. Such is the attraction of this camp for the poor that the local government has found it necessary to stipulate that at least 51 percent of an occupant's income must be from agriculture, but this rule is not rigorously enforced. In any case, Linelle Camp has by no means evolved into "the better end" of Farmersville.

If the socioeconomic complexion of Linelle Camp has not altered appreciably, the physical demeanor is considerably changed. Like Cumberland, the geographic boundaries and the basic layout of the utilities, including roads, have persisted. For the sake of efficiency and economy of space the corners of the awkward double hexagon, which became the standard format for the camps, have been rounded out; otherwise the repetitive street pattern offers sport for dragsters (fig. 94). The manager's office occupies what was once the store and post office. The washhouse is gone, the clinic is now a residence, but the community building still survives and even fulfills its original purpose. The biggest loss has been the central park area, which was covered over with some of the hundred concrete block apartments that provided alternative housing when the original metal huts were torn down in 1968. Several years later the two-story wooden apartments were also scuttled and replaced with concrete

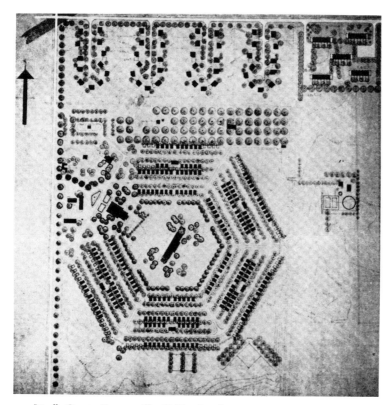

94. *Linelle Camp, Farmersville, California, plan, ca. 1937.*

triplexes. With buildings mushrooming to take up greater and greater amounts of space, a small, drab auxiliary area was drafted as the open area. The overall effect is of a pincer operation with one serried row of buildings closing in on the other.

The number of units has remained about the same; however, the apartments are a great deal more spacious than they once were. The sacrificial victim was the central park, designed by landscape architect Garrett Eckbo at the start of his career. Eckbo used Linelle Camp as a weapon in his challenge to the landscape status quo by including it and other of his Farm Security Administration work in his seminal book of 1950, *Landscape for Living* (fig. 95). His free-form design taunted the tired symmetry and rigid containment of the Renaissance-derived compositions that had monopolized landscape design through the Depression. On fields like lowly Linelle's, young landscape architects like Garret Eckbo, who had begun his revolt in school, now threw down the gauntlet against the Beaux Arts.

Linelle's significance is incongruous because it is now, as it has always been, the most unassuming of settlements. Its one tolerable area, now that the original park space has been usurped, is the band of forty-eight "garden cottages," the only section where a few original residents still hold out. Here the cul-de-sac and the subsistence garden make a last, brave stand (fig. 96). Here in a 1940 migrant labor camp in California, the Garden City movement that emanated from England in the early 1900s comes to a humble close. The movement lay dormant for almost a quarter of a century, reemerging in the plans for Reston, Virginia and Columbia, Maryland.

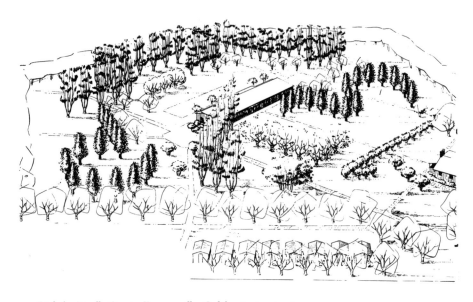

95. Park for Linelle Camp, Farmersville, California, perspective, ca. 1937.

96. Linelle Camp, Farmersville, California, Garden Cottages. Drawing by Madelaine Gill Linden.

Physical alterations in the three New Deal colonies paralleled a decline in community fiber. At Linelle, the clinic, the store, the post office, the washhouse, and the librarian once stationed in the recreation center departed. Only day-care, some religious and recreational activities, and the water and sewerage system remained. At Homestead the cooperative cannery, the store, and other shared ventures all failed. By 1948 the last of the collective businesses collapsed at Greendale. The few peppers and tomatoes still growing at Linelle and the leased bean fields at Cumberland are vestiges of the hopes for agricultural integration, if not total self-sufficiency. The New Deal planners, driven by utopian visions, were not content with the surface aspect of communities. The subject populations, however, did not share their hubris or desire to put forth the effort to keep an anomalous, collective enclave going. Looking back upon a long career that involved much work in public housing, an interest and expertise first acquired with the Farm Security Administration, architect Vernon De Mars commented that he had concluded that despite the best plans of visionary designers, people do not want to be different.[22] The evolution toward conformity at these three New Deal communities supports this thought.

Inevitably the pioneer public housing ventures of the New Deal exerted a strong influence on postwar projects. Much of this influence was of a reactive nature. For instance, in the 1950s Vernon De Mars, the former District Director of the Farm Security Administration, decided that, in order to alleviate the shame associated with public housing, he would execute a public housing complex that would look like a private development. Variations in color, floor plans, detailing, and siting would allow it to emerge from the disciplined, uniform ranks of buildings that were characteristic of the migrant labor camps, but especially of the plans of the PWA Housing Division. The result—Easter Hill Village in Richmond, California—was much praised. However, subsequent evaluation by Clare Cooper-Marcus revealed that in the tenants' minds the indelible, demeaning reality of public housing negated the architect's noble intention.[23] The occupants' morale was not significantly better than that of PWA project residents.

Cumberland and Greendale are in a separate class from PWA housing, farm labor camps, and such latter-day projects as Easter Hill Village. The rural subsistence homesteads and the greenbelt towns expressed a zeal to remake society. Despite careful selection of just the right poor, the futurist endeavors fell flat. Yet, in view of the ignominious place occupied by public housing in our fiercely capitalist society, the bold collective experiments did succeed, if not in leading the nation towards cooperative canneries and communal chicken flocks, at least in ennobling the whole concept of government-owned housing by bestowing upon it a purpose beyond mere rehabilitation or charity. That many people remained in these towns—after eleven years each could boast that it retained half of its original population—confirms that these were settlements with a sense of self-respect. If respect and emulation could be priced, then the fourteen million Depression dollars invested in Cumberland and Greendale were well spent.

From a political vantage these communities—aberrations in a pattern of modern American settlement—reflect the infrequent phenomenon of an intellectual theory that becomes reality. As with the more innovative New Deal programs like the Shelterbelt or the TVA, popular respect for authority, not Schlesinger's "malaise," made these dissident housing ventures possible. This was a society, after all, that moved quietly out of the way of parkways and signed up in an orderly mass for the WPA and the CCC. This was also a surprisingly homogeneous culture that uniformly subscribed to *The Saturday Evening Post* and flocked to the latest Ginger Rogers and Fred Astaire film. Stratified yet unified, from the President on down, the United States of the thirties could with one mind yearn for the log cabin in the woods and admit of the importance and beauty of a rose garden in a public park.

CHAPTER TEN

The Tennessee Valley Becomes a New Deal Aerie

BY UNSTINTING application of its faith in planning, the Roosevelt forces provided the impetus that moved the Tennessee Valley into the modern industrial era in advance of the rest of the South. As the valley rose from obscurity to stardom, the Tennessee Valley Authority, the powerful coordinating agency that masterminded its evolution, gained world reknown. In planning annals the TVA acquired deific status. And, like many deities, this colossus has been much acclaimed but little understood. A study of the valley reveals that, despite all the kudos, the TVA was in many ways a disappointment. In general, the New Deal planners, apart from their quixotic reforestation on the plains and idealized community-building, had stepped cautiously on the land. In the Tennessee Valley, however, they marched boldly ahead. The planners envisioned a nine-hundred-mile-long "laboratory in social and economic life."[1] The TVA first envisioned a giant network of greenbelt-style communities. Before these plans could even spark, political antagonism defused them. Today, only one small new town and the once-innovative road that leads to it betoken their abortive hopes.

The size and scope of the TVA guaranteed that it was to become a compendium of the planning rubric of the day. It had every landscape device but a national park. That it didn't need, because it *was* a national park, not of canyons, flumes, or domes, but of planning techniques, technical advances, and even some social experiment. The TVA symbolized the faith of the day in planning, and the successes and failures of the Tennessee Valley still define the potential and limitations of grandiose social and economic design.

Initially Congress was so eager and so unconcerned with the consequences that it gave the Tennessee Valley Authority carte blanche to manage **133** an area approximately the size of Ohio. The TVA river basin runs for nine hundred miles through seven states (fig. 97). The mandate of the TVA covered navigation, flood control, reforestation, marginal lands, agriculture, and industry. In addition, two critical sections of the May, 1933 legislation allowed the conducting of "studies, experiments, or demonstrations" suitable to furthering the TVA's larger goals and encouraged activity that would promote the "economic and social well-being of the people living in said river basin." As Arthur Morgan, the first chairman of the Tennessee Valley Authority, aptly remarked, "Congress didn't give us very precise instructions. They said: Here is the Tennessee Valley; go to it."[2]

Roosevelt's appointment of Arthur Morgan to the chairmanship confirms the President's missionary intent; Morgan, an engineer with extensive experience stabilizing Ohio's Miami River, was a visionary. He came to the TVA job from the presidency of Antioch College, where he had established the policy, still observed today, of mingling academics and practical work experience. Morgan sought as his chief planner a person who would be sympathetic with his goals and would not challenge his leadership. Much to the frustration of Lewis Mumford, Morgan elevated Earle Draper, a relatively obscure figure, to the position of director of the TVA's Division of Land Planning and Housing. Draper, a protegé of John Nolen, brought to the position his considerable background in planning and landscape architecture in the South. Not associated with the regional and city planning efforts around New York, Draper was a safe, noncontroversial figure to lead an experimental planning venture.[3]

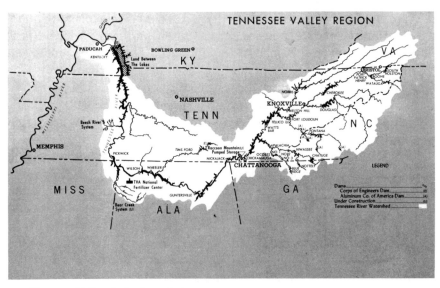

97. Tennessee Valley Authority region, 1973.

As director, Earle Draper raised the discipline of landscape architecture to its apex of power. Within a short time, sixteen to twenty other landscape architects were working with Draper, who commanded as well architects, engineers, social scientists, planners, and geographers, all dedicated to the task of propelling the forty-one thousand square miles of the Tennessee Valley into the twentieth century. Draper did not have time to oversee such day-to-day details of the operation as the building of the new town of Norris. For this he hired his colleague, landscape architect Tracy Augur. The TVA brought to fruition the future that Henry Hubbard had envisioned when he announced that landscape architects were "a force worth considering in the affairs of the country."

The TVA represented the culmination of the landscape architects' early initiative in planning. Indeed, landscape architects established the discipline of city planning. Frederick Law Olmsted, Jr. was in 1917 one of the two co-founders of the American City Planning Institute. Landscape architects comprised the largest single group in the Institute's membership.[4] For his part, Henry Hubbard not only editorialized about his profession; he also inaugurated a journal devoted to city planning and, in 1929, instituted at Harvard the nation's first full curriculum in planning. Hubbard's efforts intensified in the thirties. By 1939 the layers of planners reached to the White House, as the National Resources Planning Board, which began as an advisory arm of the PWA, was incorporated into the Executive Office itself. In 1935, two journals devoted to the profession—*Planning and Civic Comment* and *The Planners Journal* (now the *American Planning Association Journal*)—came into existence. Howard K. Menhinick, Director of Planning at the TVA, and the indefatigable Henry Hubbard originated the latter publication. It featured technical information geared toward the growing circle of professional planners.

Although the appearance of the two journals indicated that the attempt to harmonize economic and social factors with the land was becoming a distinct profession, landscape architects composed almost a third of the consultants advising the forty-two State Planning Boards that had sprung up with the guidance of the National Planning Board.[5] The discipline of planning advanced far under the aegis of the New Deal, but it still leaned heavily upon the older tradition of landscape architecture. In its turn the American Society of Landscape Architects harbored enough expertise both to tend its own garden and to nurture the grand schemes of the planners.

The development of this field during the Depression decade was marked by the rise of State Planning Boards and the National Resources Planning Board. But the spiritual home of the discipline was the Tennessee Valley Authority. The TVA officials found themselves to be sought-after public figures. Earle Draper churned out articles for the various journals, consulted with other agencies like the Resettlement Administration, and traveled as far as Washington State to address planning groups. The American Society of Landscape Architects featured Arthur Morgan as the principal speaker at its annual meeting in 1934. As stated, the Director of Planning became the first editor of the prestigious *Planners Journal*. The TVA became a cynosure for delegations of visitors who wanted to see the giant experiment-in-progress. The American Society of Foresters held their annual meeting at Knoxville in 1934. The National Conference on State Parks convened at Norris in 1938. From abroad came such distinguished visitors as the eminent British biologist Julian Huxley, Sir Raymond Unwin, architect for the archetypal garden city of Letchworth, and Sir Geoffrey Jellicoe. According to Earle Draper, the Tennessee Valley experiment was more respected in Europe than in America.[6]

Whether European or American, observers of the Tennessee Valley have always tended to impose upon the expansive events there their own peculiar visions. Julian Huxley, writing in 1944 when England stood alone in Europe against Fascism, hailed the venture as an "outstanding example of democratic planning." The 1976 *Encyclopedia of Urban Planning* touts the TVA as "the earliest example of federal legislation for planning in its modern sense," while Norman Newton in his history of landscape architecture lauds the endeavor as "the greatest single landscape architecture project on record."[7] Because of its enormity and its beatific status in architectural history, the project has defied more reasoned treatment.

While remarkable, the achievement of the Tennessee Valley Authority does not always deserve the congratulations. Consider the claim that it represented "democratic planning." On the contrary, the New Deal administration accomplished the quantity of public work that it did precisely because the process was *not* democratic. Rather, the blueprint was all-powerful. Robert Moses and his 9 parkways and 255 parks support this fact. On a more regional scale, the Blue Ridge Parkway charted a relatively untroubled and triumphant course. Yet according to a 1936 government estimate, at least four families were dislodged for every mile of roadway built. The same commentary notes that even the usurption of a few acres was seriously disruptive to families. Ironically, this criticism did not appear outside the government.[8] Nationally, the parkway was considered a boon to the area it traversed. In the Tennessee Valley the manner of development underscores the unassailable authority of the architectural or engineering drawing. Norris Dam, the first of the megalithic TVA dams, and its issue, Norris Lake, displaced roughly thirty-five hundred people. Transpose this project to a more recent time, and imagine the protest rallies the plans would inspire.

Norris Lake buried a town, but the protest was insignificant. In its own tribute, the TVA commissioned Lewis Hine to document graphically the threatened landscape. One image, "Washday at Stooksberry," has since gained some reknown (fig. 98). Even more moving than the heroic images captured by Hine is a volume of amateur photographs by Marshall Wilson, a

98. Lewis Hine, "Washday at Stooksberry," 1933.

local man hired by the TVA to assist in relocating the uprooted population.[9] As a self-appointed commentator on the imminent flood, Wilson described the affected people's reactions: "This rapid and, to some, shocking transition to a new era was pleasing only to a very few of the disrupted persons but the resentment of most was ameliorated by hopeful promises of progress following the Great Depression."

This brief account is revealing in more ways than one. During the Depression era it was a long way from Capitol Hill or Beacon Hill to Stooksberry. Authority was more respected; the deprived segment of the population more desperate. Even if it were so inclined the poor majority was too weak and disorganized to oppose the will of the Government. Nor did it have much to surrender. In the place of penury and backwardness, Washington held out the vision of a domesticated, mobilized world. Ignorance, helplessness, compliance, and optimism all facilitated the rise of the contemporary landscape.

Still, those who were disowned by the industrialization and commercialization of the Tennessee Valley would hardly have concurred with Julian Huxley that the chain of events represented the "outstanding example of democratic planning." And if "planning in its modern sense" implies a process of advocacy and consensus, then the *Encyclopedia of Urban Planning*'s summation of the TVA falls flat too. Norris Dam was topped off, in good New Deal fashion, a scant three years after it was conceived. Tellico Dam reflects the contrasting pace and power of modern planning. Begun in 1967, Tellico Dam was not completed until 1979, principally because the river housed a rare colony of snail darters. The dam displaced only 341 families, but so controversial was the whole undertaking that the eviction in 1979 of the obstinate last two merited national attention. The TVA empire could not be built today.

From 1933 to 1941 the TVA built an efficient hydroelectric grid, including nine major lakes. It also established a new town, seven rustic parks, a "freeway," and six progressive labor camps. It stimulated thousands of acres of reforestation and initiated a major fertilizer industry as well as a broad program of agricultural reform. Still, its planners were disappointed. The Tennessee Valley venture had been launched with the illusion that the golden era of planning had arrived. In his 1933 Message to Congress, in which he introduced the concept of the TVA, Roosevelt expressed his personal faith in planning. He bemoaned the helter-skelter course of growth in the nation's past and proclaimed it "time to extend planning to a wider field." In the *Planners Journal* Earle Draper outlined the ways in which planning would engage problems at all levels. "There must be no gaps," he insisted.[10] In his address to the annual assemblage of landscape architects, Morgan cited the need for a philosophy of social planning and organization. He proposed to begin by tackling the practical problems of erosion and unemployment. From this base the larger aims would follow.

Morgan brought to the TVA the reform zeal that had led him to improve the living conditions of the laborers under his charge on the Ohio River control project. At the TVA, Morgan transformed the normally mundane labor of building a dam. In order to work on Norris Dam, forty thousand prospective laborers took a special exam. Those hired worked only five and a half hours a day in order to maximize the size of the work pool and, more important, to permit the workers to take part in supplementary training. In his leisure time the TVA hod carrier could improve himself by learning woodworking, ironmongering, automobile repair, or the pasteurization of milk, in addition to participating in assorted cultural activities. Morgan advanced the Jeffersonian ideal of the proficient, informed citizen in contact with the land. The TVA, like the CCC, the Subsistence Homesteads, and the Resettlement Administration, may not have attained its lofty citizen, but its methods, like those of its brethren, foreshadowed the modern adult education movement.

The town of Norris near the dam also promoted the self-sufficiency motif. Applicants were screened to select those willing to engage in home industry or agricultural projects. The town even boasted a collective farm.

In fact, of all the New Deal communities, Norris is the best representative of thirties planning ideology. Tracy Augur commanded the show under Draper's guidance. Open space supersedes architecture in Norris—a generous greenbelt still girdles the town. Norris proves Albert Mayer's theory that the greenbelts of the era were too wide for the settlements they encompassed.

Encircled by forest and lacking easy access to the highway with its fast food franchises and automobile dealers, Norris seems stranded in the woods, cut off from the pulse of civilization.

The autocracy of the landscape prevails within the village as well. The nondescript "indigenous" houses retire behind broad setbacks. The circuitous roads submit modestly to the existing contours of the land (fig. 99). The outsized, amorphous town common sprawls at the center of the community. Buffered and bedecked with vegetation, Norris is today a popular place to live and, aptly, it is headquarters to the TVA's environmental department, the Division of Land and Forest Resources.

Norris never fulfilled its mission as a prototype community. The demise of the idea of a network of "cooperative colonies" in the true greenbelt style keenly distressed the Division of Land Planning and Housing.[11] The removal of Arthur Morgan in 1938 did much to undermine the TVA aesthetic; a Supreme Court decision two years earlier had done even more. By only one vote the Court had approved the Authority's right to distribute power at the local level. This narrow endorsement of what had been presumed a basic right of the Authority pulled the Division of Land Planning and Housing up sharp, forcing it to limit its excursions into social and economic redevelopment.

A new atmosphere of caution curtailed the activities of the agency's landscape architects, who now had to assume either advisory or covert roles.

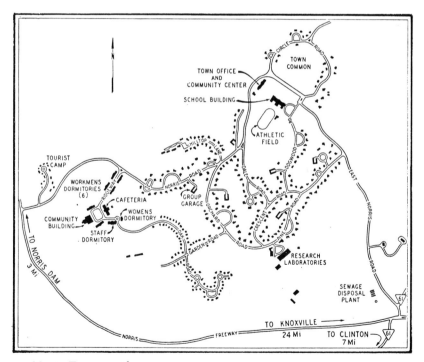

99. Norris, Tennessee, plan, 1933.

As an example of the former, the TVA sponsored the establishment of the subsistence town of Cumberland, then participated in its genesis by making inspection trips and filing reports with the Resettlement Administration. On the covert side, Harold Frincke recalls doing many subdivision plans of surplus TVA land in order to encourage its purchase by private interests. Earle Draper states that the Division did a great deal of collaborative design work with local authorities without benefit of the TVA letterhead.[12] Local entities lacked technical expertise, so they naturally drew heavily on the resources, especially the sixteen landscape architects, of the Division of Land Planning and Housing.

This curtailment of the TVA's broadest ambitions did not forestall all original landscape work. Earle Draper and his associates made notable contributions to the evolution of the modern landscape. Thematically, the most outstanding development affecting the land was the dissolution of the line between facilities for recreation and work. Harold Frincke, after a lifetime with the TVA, stresses the revolutionary nature of the whole concept of public access to a federal project. In the past, the Army Corps of Engineers had always fenced off its installations. In contrast, the TVA not only made dams accessible, but encouraged public visitors by building facilities for them. For this effort, TVA ownership and control of the littoral land was a requirement. Prior to the TVA's move to establish a public claim to the recreational benefits of its lakes, the standard procedure was to acquire only to normal water level and take easements on land above that. Earle Draper proudly points to this expansion of the public perimeter as his principal accomplishment at the TVA.[13] Given this mandate, the TVA designers displayed considerable ingenuity in turning borrow pits into marinas, crane sites into overlooks, and construction camps into tourist villages.

In consequence, when the state park officials convened at Norris in 1938, they were able to tour not just a dam and a lake, but two overnight camps and the vaunted Big Ridge Park. This project involved the work of ten CCC camps to impound a long arm of Norris Lake by means of a secondary fifty-foot dam. To arrive at Norris, the delegates travelled on the world's first utilitarian, limited-access road. A workaday road in parkway garb, the Norris Freeway epitomized the blending of commerce and recreation in the Tennessee Valley. Tractor-trailers and Norris residents could enjoy all the perquisites of a parkway: seventy-five-foot setbacks, plantings, and reduced congestion. Today, except for the few miles near the dam, only an inexplicably wide stretch of open land between the road and its contiguous buildings reminds us that Tennessee Route 441 was once a byway of international repute. Norris Lake, with its new town, parks, and innovative freeway inaugurated a pattern that might well have been replicated had the Supreme Court more firmly endorsed TVA power.

Even before the Supreme Court decision the Tennessee Valley Authority had to struggle to define the nature and limits of its engagement with the land. At Norris Lake, the TVA bought the whole watershed up to the top of the surrounding hills. In succeeding projects, it restricted itself to a land buffer of one-fourth to one-eighth of a mile. This compromise entailed a host of questions endemic to the issue of public weal versus private right. Should the TVA take eighty acres of a man's farm and leave him with a useless twenty? On the other hand, rather than go to the expense of building an access road, why not buy a whole block of land? Exactly how much land did recreation require? These issues still plague conservation annexations. With its imperial mandate not only to preserve the land but to revive agriculture and silviculture, the TVA was tempted to large-scale acquisition. If it had directly controlled large areas of land, the Authority could have singlehandedly implemented re-forestation and anti-erosion practices. By confining itself to ownership only of a modest border around its lakes, the TVA opted in the areas of agriculture and forestry for a pedagogical rather than a proprietary course.

This decision strengthened the case for recreation. The narrow lakeside property lent itself to leisure purposes. As a result, the Authority owned and managed park sites for purposes of demonstration, but never directly controlled farm land or forest. The landscape architect, not the farmer, the developer, or the forester, would arbitrate the future. TVA's Division of Agriculture greeted with dismay the ascendancy of the Division of Land Planning and Housing, which came about as a result of this policy. But neither farmers nor planners anticipated the heights to which recreation would rise. Sir Raymond Unwin alone seems to have had an inkling of the important place recreation would eventually hold in the Valley. Upon the occasion of his visit in the early days of the TVA, Unwin predicted that the lakes would one day surpass in significance the hydroelectric power they produced.[14] He did not go so far as to forecast that recreation would become the premier industry in the Valley. In fact, so dramatically has recreation eclipsed agriculture that in its contemporary theme park, Land Between the Lakes, the TVA includes a model farm to instruct visitors on the self-proclaimed, important—but no longer visible—role of the farm in our society.

Earle Draper and his cohorts chafed at the restriction on the Authority to create demonstration projects only. Gradually the Division of Land Planning had to cede its various parks, marinas, and campsites to state or private control. After establishing the principle of public right of access to government-owned lakes and facilities, the TVA influence in recreation waned.

Compared with other of its several statutory mandates the TVA's performance in silviculture has had little national repercussion. Forestry in the Tennessee Valley has conformed to general trends. Here, as elsewhere during the thirties, forestry concentrated on plantations and forest fire control, the difference being one of degree rather than of purpose. The national mania for tree-planting surfaced here in the form of two giant nurseries doling out 153 million seedlings, while twenty-four CCC camps planted enough of them to cover about a quarter of the valley. Here the blight of erosion rather than the opportunity for commercial gain motivated the reforestation drive. TVA-commissioned photographers documented the dramatic results, little realizing that they were recording the makings of the chief forest industry in the valley today (figs. 100, 101). The abundant evidence these plantations of the thirties offered of what a pine could do in fifteen years was a critical factor in the decision of a giant paper company to locate in the area in the fifties.[15]

Since the war the TVA has been very much conscious of the commercial potential of a twenty-one-million-acre forest coverage. Starting with pamphlets boosting hardwood manufacture in the forties and fifties, the agency has actively encouraged the development of a regional forest industry and ensured its viability by sponsoring new waves of planting. In the seventies the Division of Forestry was subsumed by a new Division of Land and Forest Resources and manpower was cut to a fifth of its previous size. As the Tennessee Valley fulfills its prophecy and becomes a diversified industrial behemoth, forestry like agriculture fades into the background.

Field agriculture, although much less prominent in the Tennessee Valley than forests, has had by itself a much greater influence. The nub of a truly global impact in agriculture is the TVA's work with chemical fertilizer, which

100. Tennessee Valley, erosion, 1933.

101. Tennessee Valley, above site reforested, several years later.

started with a surplus dam and two defunct government munitions factories which were converted to the production of fertilizer. Unable to get a decent price for the complex at Muscle Shoals, Alabama, the TVA started the National Fertilizer Development Center. Subsequently the Muscle Shoals plant virtually revolutionized fertilizer usage in this country and abroad.

The development and proselytization of chemical fertilizer became the linchpin of TVA agriculture. In part to promote its chemical fertilizer, the TVA originated the test or demonstration farm. Adopted by the Soil Conservation Service, these farms spread as far as LaCrosse, Wisconsin and Magnum, Oklahoma. Even without the example of the government-supported test farm, word of mouth alone would have eventually sold the rest of the nation and the world on TVA fertilizer. The TVA today boasts that "most U.S. fertilizers are made with the aid of TVA technology."[16]

Dispenser and promoter of technology, the TVA was and is still the ultimate Watershed Demonstration Area. It inspired seventy-five self-styled projects across the country during the thirties, as well as a succession of domestic and foreign river development projects, beginning with the Bonneville Dam and the Columbia River in Oregon. By the early fifties the TVA had brought a comforting degree of prosperity to the Valley, and by the late seventies it had raised the average per capita income there from the 1929 level of 45 percent of the national average to a more acceptable 79 percent. Pleasure boats busily plied the lakes. New industries and docking facilities dotted lakeshores. Intensively fertilized fields sprouted alfalfa, servicea, and winter legume. After thirty years of Authority sway the forest industry was valued at a half-billion dollars annual production.[17] Although frustrated in many of their ambitions the TVA planners had taken great strides toward securing the "economic and social well-being of the people living in said river basin."

Yet by the end of the sixties the TVA had become anathema to the liberal element of the population, the selfsame sector that had endorsed its rise. In an age of revolt against technology and monopoly the TVA represented the antithesis of a new conservation ethic. In its continuing aggrandizement of technology, it was energetically strip-mining its hills, leading the way in the two suspect areas of nuclear power and chemical fertilizer, and disrupting the habitat of the snail darter. When wild rivers began to win the praise formerly given to harnessed ones, the TVA was still building blockbuster dams. The Clinch River Breeder Reactor was a far cry from the harmonious nexus of versatile, self-sufficient communities connected by parkways and surrounded by open land that was the dream of the old Division of Land Planning and Housing. The mythic status of the TVA was disintegrating.

Despite its lapses the TVA still symbolizes for the world the possibilities of coordinated regional planning. While its deficiencies have garnered it national attention and its strengths have accrued it national neglect, the world-at-large persists in flocking to its door. From the beginning, as Earle Draper ruefully observed, the TVA's main impact has been not domestic but foreign. Undeveloped areas seeking to modernize still emulate it. In 1952 the Authority compiled a list of countries around the world that had prepared development projects modeled after its own. The list comprised thirty-six nations, almost half of which had hired former TVA staff for their work. In 1951 eighteen hundred visitors from sixty different countries visited the TVA.[18] As recently as 1984, the agency claimed nine hundred visitors from abroad. So New Deal ideals still live—at least in the Mahanadi Valley of India.

From the United States' vantage, much the TVA does is no longer unique. Large utilities now as a matter of course balance conservation, recreation, and social issues. Other governmental agencies, like the Forest Service Experimental Stations or the Department of Energy, are making the breakthroughs in land and building research. Nonetheless, the TVA still stands quite alone in the breadth of its concerns; the wide scope of its mandate gives it freedom to act and the potential for future innovation.

A Final Inspection

WHEN FRANKLIN ROOSEVELT was first toying with the idea of a Presidential retreat, he imagined a woodland setting in which the President and Cabinet members would occupy separate cabins and then assemble for meals in a common dining room. Since Harold Ickes could not stand Secretary of Treasury Henry Morganthau or Postmaster James F. Farley or WPA Director Harry Hopkins, the Cabinet members undoubtedly had other ideas for their vacations. In the end the Cabinet did not have to worry. FDR's retreat, when it finally materialized, did not return to the Boy Scout paradigm. But even though FDR did not perfect his communal resort, the concept is a telling footnote to New Deal history.

First of all, like FDR's communal dining hall, much that issued from the Depression years seems fanciful. Second, from rose garden to prairie woodland to kudzu, a powerful yearning for the past and for stability and order fueled the tremendous productivity of those poignant years. To achieve harmony the nation grasped for the old—the pioneer, the colonial, the Renaissance—but was also willing to venture the new—the greenbelt town and the Shelterbelt. The common effort of many people allied in one or more often ad hoc organizations did establish a far-reaching stratum of solid, lasting, and appealing constructions on the land. Moreover, a buoyant confidence in the cooperative spirit contributed to the founding of such experimental associations as the Tennessee Valley Authority and the various subsistence homesteads and greenbelt towns.

Romantic as it was, the fantasy of the New Deal was of a very different nature than the sensuous ideal and refinements of the preceding twenty years, **145** which produced the lushness of Art Nouveau and the eccentricities of the Arts and Crafts movement. The aesthetic of the thirties reflects a cultural epoch stripped of narcissism. The plain but omnipresent public building evokes the mass concentration of effort that was put forth to combat the turmoil of the time. The economic vicissitudes limited personal or intellectual indulgence. The nature of the nationwide employment program reinforced the tendency toward austerity, and the nostalgia for the formative years of this country which characterized both the writing and the building of the Depression era evoked an aesthetic that suited the economic conditions of a surplus of hand labor and a dearth of capital.

Forces outside economics also shaped the populist image of thirties art and architecture. The period's literature demonstrates the same tendency as its architecture toward a mass aesthetic. Warren Susman cites the plays of William Saroyan and Clifford Odets, which inclined toward sentimentality and anti-intellectualism.[1] Their penchant toward an identification with mass culture parallels the architectural trend, as rustic shelters and water cascades were being transferred from an elite culture to a mass one. Moreover, both sentimentality and anti-intellectualism also describe the "Daniel Boone" ambience of the park and forest work or the Villa Lante aspirations of municipal park development. In his final analysis of thirties literature Susman refers to the speech in *The Maltese Falcon* in which Sam Spade says to Brigid O'Shaughnessey that he will have to turn her in because she has murdered his partner, but he will wait for her. Susman characterizes this farewell as "hard

102. Aquatic Park, Berkeley, California.

103. Mt. Diablo State Park, California, museum/tower.

yet romantic; pragmatic yet with rigid adherence to a special code of belief and values; commonplace yet strangely elevated in mood."[2] If Sam Spade had made this speech at Berkeley's Aquatic Park or New York's Carl Schurz Park, rhetoric and setting would have been in accord (fig. 102).

Two tower buildings built twenty to twenty-five years apart evoke the contrast of the hard yet romantic, pragmatic but committed New Deal artifacts with the elegant, self-satisfied creations of an earlier time (figs. 103, 104). The combined museum and tower building on top of the mountain in Mt. Diablo State Park in Northern California was built in the late thirties by CCC veterans of the Spanish–American War and World War I (fig. 103). Fortress-like in appearance, its main refinement is the octagonal shape of the fenestrated tower, the eight corners of which face the eight directions of the compass. Compared to the plain mass of the Mt. Diablo structure, the 1917 Crown Point View House set along the Columbia River Highway is a riot of detail (fig. 104). The circular shape of the multistepped stone pedestal base sets a tone of elegance. The structure's stone surface is finished and subtly differentiated by plinths, architraves, buttresses, and groupings of attached columns. The fine domed roof made of lead, so different from the demure octagonal cap of the Mt. Diablo tower, completes the luxuriant image. The interior, ablaze with marble, is even more opulent than the exterior. It is clearly not the handiwork of a hastily-assembled group of unemployed veterans.

Crude by comparison, the Mt. Diablo summit building possesses its own

104. Columbia River Highway, Oregon, Crown Point View House, built in 1917. Drawing by Madelaine Gill Linden.

intrinsic dignity. Indeed, the rudest rock outhouse from the Depression speaks as eloquently of its day as the more ornate Crown Point structure does of its more prosperous era. The Mt. Diablo lookout conveys some of the earnestness, didacticism, and stoicism that typifies the art and architecture of many Western nations during the prewar period. In painting, sculpture, and architecture, heroic figures and massive structures with heavy, simple contours plant themselves firmly in defiance of disarray (fig. 105). At once an escape and an act of reaffirmation, the art is above all else political. The thirties was a time of groups, political parties, and mass assemblages dedicated to putting an end to the economic and social turbulance. The resulting landscape reflects the pangs of this "crisis of the old order."

In the United States, although the gears of the great industrial mechanism born of the eighteenth and nineteenth centuries may have temporarily slipped, technology revolutionized the countryside. The landscape of a new age was eclipsing that of the old. Great bridges (the Triborough, the Golden Gate, and the Oakland–Berkeley Bay Bridge), mighty roads (the Blue Ridge and Henry Hudson Parkways, the Pennsylvania Turnpike), and giant dams (the Hoover, the Bonneville, the TVA dams) transformed the new terrain into a landscape of mobility and industrialization. The Depression, along with natural disasters, loosed a horde of transients and rural refugees onto the nation's increasingly crowded thoroughfares. The federal government, with its truckloads of WPA workers and CCC boys, was not only a maker, but one of the biggest users of the roads. The automobile, whose sales continued to boom despite the vagaries of the economy, further increased the highway population. In the face of the advance of roads, parkways, parks, and other leisure facilities, the traditional landscape of small farms and villages began to recede.

105. Grant Wood, Seed Time & Harvest. *(Collection of Whitney Museum of American Art, New York; Gift of Arthur G. Altschul, 1937.)*

Nevertheless, although the new mobility was both novel and perceptible, its volume and velocity were still small in comparison to what future eras would bring. Whereas six million tourists visited the national parks in 1936, forty-five million flocked to them in 1970.[3] The comparatively modest proportions of New Deal roads, parking lots, and buildings represented the beginnings of the mobile lifestyle of today.

Technology and scientific discovery may have advanced the cause of the tourist, but for some time the farmer remained unenlightened. Farming practices were ruinously ignorant. Indeed, the deplorable condition of arable land finally forced a reappraisal of traditional agricultural practices in this country. The cause of soil conservation then became a major part of the general conservation movement that gained momentum during the Depression era.

The Sierra Club would not recognize as conservation work what was done under that name during the thirties. The zealous blasting of fire roads and the enthusiastic damming of rivers ordered the environment in the name of a different conservation ethic than prevails today. Yet the concept of ecology, although not as popular, did exist. Aldo Leopold, who in 1949 penned *The Sand County Almanac,* the classic in the field of ecology, commended the Soil Conservation Service for its work in the La Crosse–Coon Creek area of his native Wisconsin. Frank Waugh preached to the National Park Service the benefits of natural succession—the yielding of dominance from one plant or plant group to another—and the preservation of wilderness habitats. Although foresters misunderstood the cause of blister rust and were blind to the need for controlled burning, they had available a great body of natural science lore. But a sense of urgency, not considered analysis, dictated the actions of the thirties. Rivers were dammed, but rivers, sometimes conduits of stench and disease, were more often forces of vast destruction. In 1936 the Merrimac, Connecticut, Hudson, Delaware, Susquehanna, Potomac, Allegheny, and Ohio rivers turned into demons. The next year a raging Ohio River drove an estimated half million people from their homes in a disaster that caused some nine hundred deaths.[4] In light of such devastation the cause of the wild river would not have found much of a following fifty years ago. The United States was a wilder place. In the thirties, conservation was not concerned with the rights of rafters and snail darters; rather, conservation often meant the protection of human life.

From field terrace and picnic shelter to ski trail and water garden, the New Deal left a panoply of monuments to itself. Public works popped up in every nook and cranny of the country. The size and scope of the undertaking guaranteed, at least in landscape architecture and in architecture, that no single model or school dominated. While Chicago and Dallas compiled worthy examples of the streamlined or moderne, in the Illinois countryside pioneer structures of log and stone emerged. Building in the Texas hinterland affected a combined Mission/ranch look. Back in New York the Beaux Arts lingered on in company with the newer fashions. No one could have toured the nation in 1935 and complained, as did one discerning traveller thirty years later at the height of the next great rash of public building, that the projects looked uniformly dull and similar.[5]

On the contrary, apart from the common trend toward simplicity and nostalgic content, the style and quality of the work varied widely. The considerable range reminds us of the broad spectrum of laborers. At one end, as evidenced by the photo of stone masons working in the Toledo Zoo, many senior and skilled craftsmen were involved (fig. 106). For the most part, however, a mass of untutored youths and men either unskilled or trained in occupations unrelated to their task composed the work force.[6] The availability of high-quality supervisors helped counteract the inexperience of the labor force, but they could not altogether expunge indifferent work. As with any vernacular design, the survival of the well-made and the disappearance of the shoddy prejudices historical evaluation.

Inferior construction has survived; some even appears in this book. The mass-produced playgrounds of New York City and the timid rose garden in Lincoln, Nebraska are two samples from widely separated areas. In New York City the WPA's own administrator decried the quality of early construction. This unlikely critic complained in the fall of 1935 that most of the projects were poor even though they had copious planning help compared to the rest of the country. Reiterating an oft-expressed theme, he blamed the WPA's failure to incorporate a competent technical staff into its administration.[7] (In fact, the nation had embarked blindly and precipitously into the contracting busi-

106. Toledo, Ohio, stone masons, ca. 1935.

ness). Gradually the WPA, along with the other fledgling New Deal agencies, became more savvy. The WPA brought an engineer into the ranks of what had been preponderately a social-work organization. This engineer, Colonel Francis C. Harrington, succeeded director Harry Hopkins upon his resignation in 1938. In the meantime, the combination of social work and construction which characterized Depression work programs proffered some spotty results. Nevertheless, if at CCC-built White Rock Lake in Dallas a picnic must take place in a bare, brown-grass setting among squat concrete grills and spindly wooden benches, the monumental spaces of Fair Park, the lush lawns and gardens of Lakecliffe Park, or the imperial stone chairs and tables of Lee Park offer welcome alternatives (fig. 107).

This weighty furniture, hunkered down in Lee Park or scattered like the ruins of a satyr's picnic along the overgrown and abandoned trails of Dallas's Revershon Park, exemplifies the most often cited criticism of crash public works programs—a tendency toward the superfluous or the anomalous. The CCC escaped this criticism because of its sacrosanct association with trees and its educational value. However, there are sufficient numbers of handsome but vacant outhouses strewn across the land to indict both the CCC and WPA on this charge. As it matured, the WPA became aware of the pitfalls of overproduction. After installing numerous ill-attended parks it finally agreed not to proceed in areas outside city, county, or state park control without first

107. Lee Park, Dallas, stone picnic furniture.

consulting the National Park Service. In San Francisco, in 1940, the WPA
went so far as to refuse to fund a Twin Peaks beautification project on the basis
that the city did not have the capacity to maintain it; though such demurrals
were rare. On the whole, rose gardens, picnic shelters, outhouses, and amphi-
theaters kept rolling out regardless of need.

Very often the need did not match the rate of manufacture. The amphitheater, a much-favored item with almost every agency but the Soil Conservation Service, appeared everywhere from the heart of a redwood forest to city
streets. Usually these governmental offerings remained empty. Then a phenomenon common to many Depression structures occurred. Twenty to thirty
years after their creation, they were discovered. The amphitheater built at
Corlears Hook as part of an ambitious urban renewal project for the Lower East
Side of Manhattan was used for the first time in 1956. After twenty-odd years
of neglect, it was here that Joseph Papp staged the first of the free summer
Shakespeare productions that have since become an integral part of Manhattan's cultural life. And according to the actors rehearsing a play the summer of
1972 in the rustic outdoor theater in Birmingham, Alabama's Avondale Park,
they were first to use that public work (fig. 108). Many other thirties fabrications have also had to wait for the crowds to catch up with them.

This phenomenon of delayed discovery has been especially true of state
parks. The 1941 national inventory of public recreation revealed that state
parks were not well attended. Even such an outstanding monument as Tim-

108. Avondale Park, Birmingham, Alabama, outdoor theater.

berline Lodge suffered from disuse. For many years this showpiece, dedicated by Roosevelt himself, stood a forlorn and disintegrating hulk. Not until the sixties did Timberline finally begin to show a profit. An official in the California state park system estimates that the public did not take full advantage of the CCC-created facilities there until the mid-1950s.[8] The New Deal creations apparently needed time to be absorbed into the mainstream.

Some still have not gained their rightful audience. A recent voyager down the Natchez Trace Parkway reported, "I was . . . on the Natchez Trace for about thirty miles; I met three vehicles and saw none parked along the road. The trace is so lonely and wild that many people don't like to use it at all."[9] Photographs of many of the Depression-built parks show them empty because much of the time they are. In Oakland, the Municipal Rose Garden, the bane of cost-cutting advocates in the city government, survives only because a volunteer crew helps maintain it. Woodminster Cascade, Oakland's other formal garden, lacking a constituency, is totally orphaned. Across the Bay, no group of devotees has come forward to mend the artificial cliffs built along San Francisco's Great Highway by National Youth Administration high school students. Now gaping holes reveal the metal armature beneath the cliffs. The Depression work is only just beginning to earn the historical recognition which fosters preservation.

Not so subject to the public whim is a different, more private landscape also influenced by the events of the FDR years. Many a home or garden betrays its owner's past experience laboring in the nation's woods and fields. Graduates of the CCC are particularly inclined to apply their skills to shaping their personal environs. One alumnus of the Civilian Conservation Corps patterned his New Jersey residence after a thirties state park—it is a country place complete with lake, beach, boating, fishing, and "lots of parking."[10] The encounter with the nation's backwoods has left its mark from Flatbush, New York to Beaverton, Oregon.

The New Deal also forged many careers in conservation and building. A great number of men associated with the CCC continued on as trustees of the nation's parks and forests. Individuals like Conrad Wirth, Harold Baker, Darcy Bonnet, William Carnes, and Sanford Hill, who spent their early career years administering the activity of the CCC, became highly placed officials in the National Parks and National Forest Services, or, in Sanford Hill's case, in the Bureau of Public Roads. No CCC enrollee has become National Park Director or Associate Director, but numerous young men from the Corps rose to the positions of Regional Forester or Park Superintendent. The Depression years also trained a generation of treetoppers, nurserymen, masons, electricians, carpenters, and other skilled tradesmen who have contributed to the contemporary landscape. Housing, soil conservation, recreation, and other land-related occupations owe a smaller but similar debt to the FDR years.

The momentum of Washington's commitment to development and conservation that began with the Depression has carried over into the modern era. Services inaugurated in those strapped years have continued in a variety of shapes and sizes. Revenue sharing, the extended Public Works Act of 1976, the Great Plains Conservation Program, the Land and Water Conservation Fund, Urban Parks and Recreation Renewal have their philosophical roots in the New Deal. In addition, the 1967 Model Cities Program, urban homesteading, new town subsidies, and other offerings of the Department of Housing and Urban Development have affected the lay of the land. Even the federalized labor forces resurface periodically. The ghost of the CCC is particularly fond of revisiting its former haunts. The first of the CCC derivatives—Job Corps—was created in 1965. It is one of the few survivors from the days of the Great Society. Three more recent revivals, less involved with labor unions, are the Youth Conservation Corps, the California Conservation Corps, and the Young Adult Conservation Corps. The seventies even exhumed the WPA in the form of the Comprehensive Employment and Training Act, or CETA. All but the California Corps expired or, in CETA's case, went into hibernation, in 1981. With a sharp recession and a sympathetic administration, they will eventually come back.

Spawned in less trying times, none of the recent derivatives of the New Deal work and construction organizations have reached the heights of their New Deal prototypes.[11] With the exception of Job Corps, the modern spinoffs have lasted only a few years. A gardener who worked under Title 2 of the Public Works Act of 1976 complained recently that much of the park planting set in by him and his compatriots died because their jobs ended before the plants had a chance to establish themselves. Title 2 lasted five years; together the WPA and its precursor the Civil Works Administration went on for nine years, ample time for a plant to take.

The same lack of continuity plagues recent conservation corps. First, only the Job Corps and the California Conservation Corps were full-time, year-round, and residential; the Youth Conservation Corps was merely a summer program. Second, none of these agencies allowed for promotion within the ranks. The original CCC had great flexibility in rewarding industry and ability by conferring "leader" or "assistant leader" rank on the enrollees. In this way the thirties outfit was able to retain workers with training and skills. Now individuals who want to stay on have to qualify for and pass the cumbersome civil service procedures.

Motivation is an even more critical factor today when a whole new breed of youth counts its blessings in Trans-Ams and stereos. The original CCC drew much of its constituency from the sons of poor urban immigrants or fourth-generation white farmers. In 1937 the average enrollee was twenty-six years old, came from a family of six children, and had completed the eighth grade.[12] Accustomed to hard work and satisfied with simple entertainment, recruits did not find the CCC lifestyle as taxing as might today's enrollee. The CCC youth brought with them skills critical to adaptation to the wilds. Even today, when they hold their reunions, these now gray-headed men display one of those skills—the fine art of story-telling. Modern youths will go into the woods, but they want to take their Trans-Ams and stereos with them.

Even assuming that a talented leadership might once more assemble, no modern public works program could replicate the best of the Depression work. It is highly improbable that an Italian Renaissance water garden will appear a second time on the Texas plains. It is equally unlikely that a group of people plopped into Pennsylvania-style houses in Eastern Tennessee will band together to raise Plymouth Rock pullets and manufacture socks. Surely the restored La Purissima Mission in California will never again witness a bunch of Brooklyn toughs crying at the prospect of leaving it. Even if labor were to become cheap again, most likely Oklahoma will never have another men's room with a ceiling made from a slab of rock ten by twelve feet and eight inches thick. Few would wish the return of this hard-pressed era, but one can pine for more of its romantic concoctions on the land.

Recreation Demonstration Areas

State	Name of Area	General Location
Alabama	Oak Mountain	Birmingham
California	Mendocino	Mendocino
Georgia	Alex H. Stephens	Crawfordville
	Hard Labor Creek	Rutledge
	Pine Mountain	Pine Mountain
Illinois	Père Marquette	Grafton
Indiana	Versailles	Versailles
	Winamac	Winamac
Kentucky	Otter Creek	West Point
Maine	Camden Hills	Camden
Maryland	Catoctin (Camp David)	Thurmond
Michigan	Waterloo	Chelsea
Minnesota	St. Croix	Hinckley
Missouri	Cuivre River	Troy
	Lake of the Ozarks	Kaiser
	Montserrat	Knobnoster
Oklahoma	Lake Murray	Ardmore
Oregon	Silver Creek	Sublimity
Pennsylvania	Blue Knob	Bedford
	French Creek	Birdsboro
	Hickory Run	Hickory Run
	Laurel Hill	Rockwood
	Raccoon Creek	Beaver
Rhode Island	Beach Pond	West Greenwich
South Carolina	Kings Mountain	York
	Cheraw	Cheraw
Tennessee	Fall Creek Falls	Pikeville
	Montgomery Bell	Burns
	Shelby Forest	Millington
Virginia	Chopawamsic	Quantico
	Swift Creek	Chester

Notes

Publication information is given for works that are not included in the bibliography.

CHAPTER ONE   THE NEW DEAL RETURN TO THE LAND

1. Olin Dows, *Franklin Roosevelt at Hyde Park* (New York: American Artists Group, 1949): 71; Rexford G. Tugwell, *FDR: Architect of an Era* (New York: Macmillan, 1967): xiv, 145; Tugwell, *In Search of Roosevelt* (Cambridge: Harvard University Press, 1972): 29. In this book Tugwell claims that Roosevelt's main legislative interest during his three years in the New York State Senate (1910–13) and his governorship, was parks and forests.

2. Bremer W. Pond, *Outline History of Landscape Architecture*, pt. 1, p. 5.

3. For the sake of simplicity and veracity the text will employ the masculine personal pronoun in reference to landscape architects. Wave Hill's inaugural conference, "American Women and Gardens, 1915–1945" (1981), and numerous recent publications have shown that women were active in the field during this period, but only a handful worked with the public sector.

4. Lewis Merriam, *Relief and Social Security*, 440.

CHAPTER TWO   THE NEW DEAL AND THE NEW PLAY

1. Hoover's pronouncement comes from the preface of the *Annual Report of the Playground Commission* (San Francisco: Playground Commission, 1928–29). Jesse Steiner wrote a second article for *The New York Times Magazine* in 1933, as well as "Recreation and Leisure Time Activities," in *Recent Social Trends in the United States;* and *Research Memorandum on Recreation in the Depression* (Washington, D.C.: Social Science Research Council, 1937).

2. The fifth edition of Butler's most popular work, *Introduction to Community Recreation*, was published in 1976.

3. Butler, *Introduction to Community Recreation*, 149.

4. Galen Cranz, in *The Politics of Park Design*, refutes the notion that the nineteenth-century park afforded only passive recreation. The WPA and its predecessor agencies had as of 1938 built 5,600 athletic fields, 12,800 playgrounds, and 3,300 variants of the grandstand and had improved or founded 8,000 parks. WPA, *Inventory: An Appraisal of the Results of the WPA* (Washington, D.C.: GPO, 1938): 19.

5. Robert A. Caro, *The Power Broker: Robert Moses and the Fall of New York,* 549; Leonard Arrington, "The New Deal in the West: A Preliminary Statistical Inquiry," 311–29.

6. L. H. Weir, ed., *A Manual of Municipal and County Parks,* 1:120. Weir asserts that "the leader is the most important and fundamental of all environmental factors" (2:110).

7. In 1983 New York City launched a $1.6 billion capital improvement program for its parks.

8. George D. Butler, ed. *The New Play Areas: Their Design and Equipment,* 187.

9. Marginal Playground #9 became the subject of national media attention since it was the intended beneficiary of the Diana Ross concert that turned into a riot in the summer of 1983.

CHAPTER THREE   THE NEW DEAL AND THE OLD WORLD

1. Frank A. Waugh, "American Ideals in Landscape Architecture," 151–54.

2. Keith Morgan's mention of Guy Lowell's *American Gardens* in his lecture "Emergence of the American Formal Garden Revival," given at the 1982 Wave Hill Conference, recalled for me the significance of that book.

3. American Society of Landscape Architects, *Illustration of Work of Members;* Abram Linwood Urban, "The Seabrook Gardens," 49–56.

4. Charles Platt, *Monograph Charles A. Platt's Work.*

5. Formerly the Oakland Municipal Rose Garden, it is now called the Morcom Amphitheater of Roses.

6. Hans J. Koehler, "Planting a Naturalistic Garden Theater in a Limestone Region," 153.

CHAPTER FOUR   THE RECREATION MIGRATION

1. U.S. Department of Commerce, Bureau of the Census, *Historical Statistics of the United States, Colonial Times to 1957* (Washington, D.C.: GPO, 1957), 14.

2. George D. Butler, ed., *Municipal and County Parks in the United States.*

3. Caro, *The Power Broker,* 508, 533; Cormier, "New York City Parks and Parkways," 124.

4. Caro, *The Power Broker,* 572. In descending order these cities were Chicago, Philadelphia, Detroit, Los Angeles, and Cleveland. New York's hyperactivity is partially explained by the fact that its population exceeded by half a million the combined total of the next three largest cities.

5. C. B. Whitnall, "Relationships of Municipal, County and State Recreation Systems," NPS, *1940 Yearbook: Park and Recreation Progress,* 34.

6. U.S. National Resources Board, *Report on National Planning and Public Works in Relation to Natural Resources Including Land Use and Water Resources with Findings and Recommendations* (Washington, D.C.: GPO, 1934), 220.

7. Gilmore Clarke, letter to the author, 2 December 1977.

8. New York Department of Parks, *Eight Years of Park Progress* (New York, 1942), 36.

9. Robert G. Hall, letter to the author, 11 June 1979. A landscape architect, Mr. Hall designed and supervised the construction of roads and bridges for the Blue Ridge Parkway.

10. Laurie Davidson Cox, "Green Mountain Parkway: The Place of Eastern Scenic Areas in a National Park System," *Parks & Recreation* 25 (September 1935): 8–11. This article, which also appeared in *LA,* described the proposed route and sounded the first public protest. *American Forests* 43 (April 1937): 186.

11. "A.S.L.A. Notes," *LA* 25 (January 1935): 99.

12. Albert C. Rose, *Historic American Roads: From Frontier Trails to Superhighways,* 96.

13. Butler, *Municipal and County Parks,* 10.

14. "Pattern for Parks," 492–509; Harold T. Groth, director of the Cleveland Metropolitan Park District, interview with the author, Cleveland, September 1972.

15. Prentiss French, interview with the author, San Francsico, 23 February 1976.

CHAPTER FIVE   RESORTING TO THE WOODS

1. Beatrice Ward Nelson, *State Recreation: Parks, Forests and Game Preserves*, 3; Frank A. Waugh, *Textbook of Landscape Gardening* (New York: John Wiley & Sons, 1922), 328.

2. Newton, *Design on the Land*, 556; U.S. Department of the Interior, *The CCC and Its Contribution to a Nation-wide State Park Recreational Program* (Washington, D.C.: GPO, 1937).

3. In an interview with the author (5 May 1977), Conrad Wirth, former director of state park planning for the CCC, claimed that the CCC did three or more times state park work than national work. NPS, *A Study of the Park and Recreation Problem of the United States*, cites the statistics on state park distribution.

4. TVA, Department of Regional Planning Studies, *Recreational Development of the Southern Highlands Region*, 17.

5. "Ickes Would Keep Parks Natural," report on an address by Harold Ickes to a convention of CCC workers in state parks, 237. Moses expresses his view of state parks in NYC Dept. of Parks, *Twenty Years of Park Progress*, 6.

6. Waugh, "American Ideals in Landscape Architecture," 153.

7. Description of the site comes from the Resettlement Administration's eligibility report as quoted in Freeman Tilden, *The State Parks: Their Meaning in American Life*, 253.

8. Ian Forbes, "The Program Demonstration at Swift Creek Recreation Area," NPS, *1938 Yearbook: Park and Recreation Progress*, 63.

9. NPS and Emergency Relief Administration, *Park Use Studies and Demonstrations*, 48.

10. Harold D. Ickes, Preface to *1940 Yearbook: Park and Recreation Progress*.

11. Carrol P. Graves, letter to the author, 26 March 1979.

12. "Buildings in the National Forest," 263–64.

13. Frank Lloyd Wright, *Modern Architecture—Being the Kahn Lectures for 1930*.

14. William D. Carnes, interview with the author, Green Valley, Arizona, 20 April 1977.

15. David Gebhard and Harriette Von Breton, *Kem Weber: The Moderne in Southern California, 1920–1941*.

16. Allyn R. Jennings, "Planning State Parks," 234.

CHAPTER SIX   THE LANDSCAPE PROFESSION IN THE DEPRESSION

1. TVA, *Development of the Southern Highlands*, 15.

2. CCC, *Recreational Development by the CCC in National and State Forests* (Washington, D.C.: GPO, 1936), 11; CCC, *The CCC and Public Recreation* (Washington, D.C.: GPO, 1941).

3. Thomas C. Vint, "National Park Service, Branch of Plans and Design, San Francisco, Office of National Parks, Buildings and Reservations," *LA* 24 (October 1933): 31–32.

4. Fon W. Boardman, Jr., *The Thirties: America and the Great Depression*, 67.

5. CCC, *Report of the Director*, 1933, 7; A. D. Taylor, "Public Works and the Profession of Landscape Architecture," *LA* 24 (April 1934): 212–14.

6. Conrad Wirth, interview with the author, Washington, D.C., 4 May 1977; William G. Carnes, interview with the author, Green Valley, Arizona, 20 April 1977.

7. Statistics for the NPS expansion appear in William C. Tweed, Laura E. Soulliere and Henry G. Law, "National Park Service Rustic Architecture: 1916–1942" (Unpublished manuscript, NPS, Western Regional Office, 1977), 92. The USFS capitulation to the landscape

profession is traced in William C. Tweed, *Recreation Site Planning and Improvement in National Forests, 1891–1942* (USFS, Washington, D.C.: GPO, 1980), 16–18.

8. William Carnes gave the figure in "Landscape Architecture in the National Park Service," 145–50.

9. Taylor, "Public Works and the Profession of Landscape Architecture," 135–41; Sanford Hill, interview with the author, Napa, California, 26 April 1979.

10. "Architectural Contracts," *Architectural Record* 74 (July 1933).

11. Charles Eliot II, interview with the author, Ipswich, Massachusetts, 6 August 1980.

12. Thomas C. Vint, "National Park Service Master Plans," 21–22; also Conrad Wirth, interview, 4 May 1977, discusses Vint's introduction of the master plan.

13. "Necrology: Minute on George Gibbs," *LA* 42 (October 1951): 27; Conrad Wirth interview, 4 May 1978.

14. William Carnes, interview, 20 April 1977.

15. Henry Hubbard, "Editorial," *LA* 22 (October 1931): 54.

16. "Phelps Wyman," *LA* 39 (April 1948): 110–11; Harold G. Fowler, *Report to the Chief Architect through the Superintendent of Sequoia National Park, California: Seasonal Report—Sixth Enrollment Period, Oct. 1, 1935–April 1, 1936* (FRC, San Francisco, RG 79, 61–A–520/31164); R. Darcy Bonnet, interview with the author, Watsonville, California, 4 April 1976.

17. Tweed, et al., "NPS Rustic Architecture," 94.

18. Philip H. Elwood, "Some Landscape Architectural Problems in Government Service," 189.

19. Melvin B. Borgeson, "Landscape Architect in Public Works: District One," 27.

20. The role of the CCC is mentioned in Department of the Interior, *Report of the Secretary* (Washington, D.C.: GPO, 1933), 157; Tweed et al., "NPS Rustic Architecture" discusses the contribution of the PWA, 76–88.

21. NPS, *1937 Yearbook: Park and Recreation Progress*, 33.

22. Earnest A. Davidson, *Emergency Conservation Work Report to the Chief Architect through the Superintendent of Mt. Rainier, 1937* (FRC, San Francisco, RG 79, 102–51/5/8953); Lloyd J. Fletcher, *Report on Building Construction*, Sequoia National Park, April 1937–April 1938 (FRC, San Francisco, RG 79, 61/A/520/31164).

23. Alfred Kuehl, interview with the author, Kentfield, California, 4 April 1976. Kuehl was the landscape architect who had to brave the mule ride down the canyon.

CHAPTER SEVEN   NOTHING SO AMERICAN

1. E. B. Nixon, ed., *Franklin D. Roosevelt and Conservation, 1911–1945*, 1:322.

2. Norman Newton, telephone interview with the author, September 1972.

3. William Carnes, interview, 20 April 1977.

4. Elwood, "Landscape Architectural Problems," 189.

5. Gilmore D. Clarke, "Notes on Texture in Stone Masonry," 197–208.

6. A. D. Taylor and R. Darcy Bonnet, "Problems of Landscape Architecture in the National Forests" (Unpublished manuscript, San Francisco: USFS Office, 1936).

7. Albert H. Good, ed., *Park and Recreation Structures*.

8. Fletcher, *Report on Building Construction*; Merriam, *Relief and Social Security*, 438; Howard Baker, interview with the author, Omaha, Nebraska, 1 September 1977; Eugene A. Howard, "Recollections on Development of the Milwaukee County Park System."

9. The best political history of the CCC is John A. Salmond's *The Civilian Conservation Corps, 1933–1942: A New Deal Case Study*.

10. Frank Thrower, architect, interview with the author, Dallas, September 1978, cites the example of Al Tufolsky, the most sought-after mason in that city. Norman B. Livermore, "Roads Running Wild," 153–55.

11. Newton Drury, interview with the author, Berkeley, 6 April 1976; George Czarnick, letter to the author 12 April 1979, describes his experience as a CCC recruit observing the powder monkeys.

12. Harold Biswell, Professor Emeritus of Forestry, University of California at Berkeley, telephone interview with the author, 28 September 1980. Fire performs a selective thinning process. Also, some conifers require fire in order to elicit the seeds from the cones; *1933 Annual, Sparta District, Civilian Conservation Corps, 6th Corps Area.*

13. Federal Security Agency, *The CCC at Work.*

14. NPS, *Director's Report, 1939,* 71.

15. Newton Drury, interview, 6 April 1976.

16. Gerald C. Wheeler, retired supervisor of the Green Mountain National Forest, letter to the author, 26 March 1979.

17. Will Iverson, Regional Landscape Architect, USFS, interview with the author, San Francisco, 1976; Gil Churchill, Information Staff Officer, Monongahela National Forest, letter to the author, 17 April 1975.

18. Lee Roberts, letter to the author, 10 April 1979.

19. NPS, *Study of the Park and Recreation Problem.*

20. George Nason, "Architecture and its Relationship to the Design of Parks," NPS, *1940 Yearbook: Park and Recreation Progress,* 57.

21. Christopher Tunnard, "Modern Gardens for Modern Houses: Reflections on Current Trends in Landscape Design," 57–68; Garrett Eckbo, letter to the author, Winter 1973.

22. Frank Waugh, "Landscape Conservation: Planning the Recreational Use of Our Wild Lands," 379–81.

CHAPTER EIGHT   THE RISE OF KUDZU AND THE SPREAD
OF THE BLACK LOCUST

1. "2,000,000,000 Seeds for Shelterbelt," 249.

2. Hugh H. Bennett, *Soil Conservation* (New York: McGraw-Hill, 1939), p. viii; "Forty Years with SCS," 12.

3. R. Burnell Held and Marion Clawson, *Soil Conservation in Perspective,* provides the basis for the discussion here.

4. For a detailed discussion of soil conservation in the plains see Donald Worster, *Dust Bowl: The Southern Plains in the 1930s.*

5. Figure 84 is from Barrett G. Potter, "The 'Dirty Thirties' Shelterbelt Project," 36–37. Reprinted from *American Forests* Magazine, January 1976.

6. For information about the Shelterbelt project I am most indebted to William H. Droze, *Trees, Prairies, and People: A History of Tree Planting in the Plains States.*

7. Paul B. Sears, "The Great American Shelterbelt," *Ecology* 17 (October 1936): 683–84, as mentioned in Droze, *Trees, Prairies, and People,* 116.

8. Telephone conversation with Art Ferber, retired SCS forester for Midwest Region, 17 January 1985, confirmed erring tree choices; Droze, *Trees, Prairies, and People,* cites the problem of incorrect orientation.

9. Joseph H. Stoeckler, *Shelterbelt Influence on Great Plain Field Environment and Crops: A Guide for Determining Design and Orientation,* U.S.D.A., Forest Service Product Research Report # 62 (Washington, D.C.: GPO, 1932), 26.

10. "Seed Collected in Large Quantities," *Soil Conservation* 1 (January 1936): 7.

11. Information from miscellaneous material in the Soil Conservation Service area office, Lincoln, Nebraska, plus telephone conversation with current SCS forester for Midwest Region, 17 January 1985.

12. Ralph A. Read, *The Great Plains Shelterbelt in 1954* (Lincoln, Nebraska: Great Plains Agricultural Council, Publication #16, 1958), 22.

13. H. D. Abbot, "C.C.C. Operations," *Soil Conservation* 3 (March 1938): 237-38.

14. Aldo Leopold, "Coon Valley: An Adventure in Cooperative Conservation," 205-08.

15. SCS, *Annual Report, Coon Creek Farm Account Work: La Crosse, Monroe and Vernon Counties, Region 9*, Ninth report (SCS, 1942). Close-crop coverage would knit down the soil; if a nitrogen-fixing legume was used, it would help restore its fertility.

16. Paul Tabor and Arthur W. Susott, "Zero to Thirty Million Mile-a-Minute Seedlings," 61.

17. Roger Thurow, "A Vine in Dixie Creeps Its Way into Infamy," *Wall Street Journal*, 24 July 1981.

18. Ann Crittenden, "Soil Erosion Threatens U.S. Farms' Output," *New York Times*, 26 October 1980.

19. Comptroller General of the United States, *Report to the Congress: Progress in Meeting Important Objectives of the Great Plains Conservation Program Could Be Improved* (SCS, Washington, D.C.: GPO, 1973).

CHAPTER NINE   REARRANGING PEOPLE ON THE LAND

1. Arthur M. Schlesinger, Jr., *The Politics of Upheaval*, 205.

2. For a detailed discussion of pre–New Deal resettlement efforts see Paul K. Conkin, *Tomorrow a New World: The New Deal Community Program*, 11-89.

3. Press release from the Division of Subsistence Homesteads, 1934 (Located in the historical files of the TVA Technical Library, Knoxville, Tennessee).

4. The other three were Westmoreland in Pennsylvania and Tygert Valley and Arthurdale in West Virginia.

5. John Nolen, "The Landscape Architect in Public Works, part II," *LA* 24 (January 1934): 82.

6. Conkin, *Tomorrow a New World*, 213.

7. Among the outside advisors sent to Cumberland was Tannis Tugwell, daughter of noted brain truster and head of the Resettlement Administration, Rexford Tugwell. Her family hastily summoned her home when she became engaged to a local boy.

8. Press release from the Division of Subsistence Homesteads, 1934.

9. Helen Bullard, "A Brief Review of Five Bulletins," *Crossville Chronicle*, 15 December 1977. Mrs. Bullard cites the pertinence of the University of Tennessee Agricultural Extension Agency studies from the period to the modern subsistence movement.

10. Amy Cox Harshman (age 90), interview with the author, Homestead, Tennessee, 6 November 1980.

11. David Myrha, "Rexford Guy Tugwell: Initiator of America's Greenbelt New Towns, 1935-1936," 176-88.

12. Lewis Mumford, *The Culture of Cities* (New York: Harcourt, Brace and World, 1938); Arnold Whittick, ed., *Encyclopedia of Urban Planning*, 1102.

13. Edna Gossage with Amy Cox and Abram Nightingale, "Cumberland Homesteads, 1933-1955," *Crossville Chronicle*, 12 July 1956, reprinted in Patricia Barclay Kirkeminde, *Cumberland Homesteads, As Viewed by the Newspapers*.

14. Albert Mayer, "Greenbelt Towns Revisited," *Journal of Housing* 24 (January–April 1967): 12-26, 80-85, 151-60.

15. Mayer, "Greenbelt Towns Revisited," pt. I (January 1967): 21; Joseph L. Arnold, *The New Deal in the Suburbs: A History of the Greenbelt Town Programs, 1935-1954*, 92.

16. Helen Bullard, "The Cumberland Homesteads: 43 Years Later," *Crossville Chronicle*, 10 November 1977. Bullard reports the findings of a 1955 headcount of Cumberland residents. Arnold, *New Deal in the Suburbs*, 236.

17. Gwendolyn Wright, *Building the Dream* (New York: Pantheon Books, 1981), 226, finds the same conservative selectivity in the PWA Housing Division. Arnold discusses the discrepancy between the poverty level and the rental costs of Greendale in *New Deal in the Suburbs*, 93, 138.

18. National Resources Planning Board, *Public Works and Rural Land Use* (Washington, D.C.: GPO, 1942), 36.

19. Vernon De Mars, interview with the author, 12 March 1981, cites Germany, and then Sweden and England, as having the principal influence on FSA housing. Talbot F. Hamlin, "Farm Security Architecture: An Appraisal," 720.

20. E. Lynn Miller, "Homesteading FDR-style at Arthurdale," 418–23.

21. Adele Carter, tenant, and Jack Dodds, manager, interview with the author, Linelle Camp, California, 22 March 1981.

22. Vernon De Mars, interview, 12 March 1981.

23. Clare C. Cooper, *Easter Hill Village: Some Social Implications of Design.*

CHAPTER TEN   THE TENNESSEE VALLEY BECOMES A NEW
DEAL AERIE

1. Arthur Morgan, "The Human Problem of the Tennessee Valley Authority," 120.

2. Tennessee Valley Authority Act, 48 *Stat.* 58 (May 1933); Morgan, "Human Problem of the TVA," 120.

3. William H. Jordy, "'A Wholesome Environment Through Plain, Direct Means': The Planning of Norris by the Tennessee Valley Authority," (1980, unpublished manuscript in the files of the chief librarian, TVA, Knoxville, Tennessee).

4. Scott, *American City Planning since 1890*, 163.

5. Charles Eliot II, interview with the author, Ipswich, Massachusetts, 6 August 1980; Henry Hubbard, "The Landscape Architect in Regional and State Planning," *LA* 25 (July 1935): 199–202.

6. Earle S. Draper, letter to the author, 30 November 1980.

7. Julian Huxley, *TVA—Adventure in Planning*, 7; Whittick, *Encyclopedia of Urban Planning*, 1094; Newton, *Design on the Land*, 646.

8. These views are reported in Mary C. Ryan, ed., *Park Service Bulletin* 6 (September–October 1936), 125382; in contrast, Bob Hall, landscape architect with the National Park Service, who worked on the road for ten years, denies seeing "any unhappiness with dispossession" (Letter to the author, 11 June 1979). Michael J. McDonald and John Muldowny's recent study, *TVA and the Dispossessed* (Knoxville, Tenn.: University of Tennessee Press, 1982) upholds the view that disruption occurred.

9. Marshall A. Wilson, "Photographs in Norris Reservoir Area," 2 vols. (TVA Technical Library, Knoxville, Tennessee). The photos were taken from 1934 to 1937; Wilson compiled the two unique volumes in 1967.

10. Earle S. Draper, "Levels of Planning," 34.

11. Earle S. Draper, "Planning Methods in the Tennessee Valley," 110.

12. Harold Frincke, telephone interview with the author, 5 November 1980; Earle S. Draper, letter to the author, 30 November 1980.

13. Earle S. Draper, letter, 30 November 1980.

14. Earle S. Draper, letter, 30 November 1980.

15. Bill Ogden, Division of Land and Forest Resources, TVA, Norris, Tennessee telephone conversation with the author, 6 November 1980, gave an updated review of TVA forestry. Howard K. Menhinick, Letter to the Editor, *Planning and Civic Comment* 12 (1946): 18–20, reported statistics regarding the CCC planting as given in the TVA's 1945 *Annual Report.*

16. TVA, "Fertilizer Research and Development," *Annual Report, 1979* (Knoxville, Tenn.: TVA, 1979), 1:51.

17. TVA, *A Short History of the Tennessee Valley Authority: 40th Anniversary of People in Partnership* (Knoxville, Tenn.: TVA, 1973), 9.

18. TVA, *TVA as a Symbol of Resource Development in Many Countries. A Digest and Selected Bibliography of Information* (Knoxville, Tenn.: TVA Technical Library, 1952).

CHAPTER ELEVEN   A FINAL INSPECTION

1. Warren I. Susman, "The Thirties," Norman Rattner and Stanley Cohen, eds., *The Development of American Culture* (Englewood Cliffs, N.J.: Prentice-Hall, 1970).

2. Ibid., 201.

3. Ben J. Wattenberg, ed., *Statistical History of the United States*, 396.

4. Frederick Lewis Allen, *Since Yesterday: The Nineteen-Thirties in America, September 3, 1929–September 3, 1939*, 167.

5. Garrett Eckbo, Preface to *Six Essays on Government and Environmental Design in the San Francisco Bay Area* (Berkeley: Institute of Governmental Studies, University of California at Berkeley, 1978), xiii.

6. According to Merriam, *Relief and Social Security*, 417, only 36.5 percent of the male workers were skilled; less than 27 percent of the semiskilled were from construction. *Final Report on the WPA, 1935–1943* (Washington, D.C. GPO, 1946), 48, states that the laborers on construction projects other than roads were generally unskilled men who were either too old for industry or too young for work experience.

7. Charles F. Searle, *Minister of Relief: Harry Hopkins and The Depression*, 155.

8. John H. Knight, telephone interview with the author, June 1976.

9. Jesse C. Mills, letter to the author, 12 December 1980.

10. Newsletter of Northeastern Region Headquarters, National Association CCC Alumni, John R. Moscinski, ed., March 1981.

11. Records through 1970 indicate that 1935 marked the pinnacle in public works expenditure for purposes of conservation and development. In 1935 the figure was 1.9 billion; the next highest figure (not adjusted for inflation) was 1.6 billion spent in 1966.

12. Salmond, *CCC: New Deal Case Study.*

Bibliography

BOOKS

Aldrich, Amey and John Walker. *A Guide to Villas and Gardens in Italy.* Rome: American Academy in Rome, 1938.

Allen, Frederick Lewis. *Since Yesterday: The Nineteen-Thirties in America, September 3, 1929–September 3, 1939.* New York: Harper & Row, 1939.

American Society of Landscape Architects. *Illustration of Works of Members.* 4 vols. New York: House of J. Hayden Twiss, 1931–34.

Arnold, Joseph L. *The New Deal in the Suburbs: A History of the Greenbelt Town Program, 1935–1954.* Columbus: Ohio State University Press, 1971.

Bachman, Earl E. *Recreational Facilities . . . A personal history of their development in the National Forests of California.* USFS: Pacific Southwest Forest and Range Experiment Station, Berkeley, California, 1967.

Boardman, Fon W., Jr. *The Thirties: America and the Great Depression.* New York: Henry Z. Walck, 1967.

Butler, George D. *Introduction to Community Recreation.* New York: McGraw-Hill, 1940.

——. *The New Play Areas: Their Design and Equipment.* NRA. New York: A. S. Barnes, 1938.

——. ed. *Municipal and County Parks in the United States.* CCC. Washington, D.C.: GPO, 1935.

Caro, Robert A. *The Power Broker: Robert Moses and the Fall of New York.* New York: Alfred A. Knopf, 1974.

Clapp, Gordon R. *The TVA: An Approach to the Development of a Region.* Chicago: University of Chicago Press, 1955.

Coffin, David R., ed. *Italian Gardens.* Washington, D.C.: Dumbarton Oaks, 1972. **167**

Conkin, Paul K. *Tomorrow A New World: The New Deal Community Program.* Ithaca: Cornell University Press, 1959.

Cooper, Clare C. *Easter Hill Village: Some Social Implications of Design.* New York: Free Press, 1975.

Cranz, Galen. *The Politics of Park Design.* Cambridge: MIT Press, 1982.

Droze, William H. *Trees, Prairies, and People: A History of Tree Planting in the Plains States.* Denton: Texas Women's University Press, 1977.

Eckbo, Garrett. *Landscape for Living.* New York: F. W. Dodge, 1950.

Fitch, James Marston. *American Building: The Forces that Shape It.* Boston: Houghton Mifflin, 1948.

Gallion, Arthur B. and Simon Eisner. *The Urban Pattern: City Planning and Design.* New York: Van Nostrand Reinhold, 1963.

Gebhard, David and Harriette Von Breton. *Kem Weber: The Moderne in Southern California, 1920–1941.* Santa Barbara: University of California at Santa Barbara, Art Galleries, 1969.

Good, Albert H., Ed. *Park and Recreation Structures.* 3 vols. NPS. Washington, D.C.: GPO, 1938.

———. *Park Structures and Facilities.* Washington, D.C.: NPS, 1935.

Gothein, Marie Luise. *A History of Garden Art.* Translated by Mrs. Archer-Hind. London: J. M. Dent & Sons, 1928.

Healy, Clyde E. *San Francisco Improved.* San Francisco: WPA, 1939.

Held, R. Burnell and Marion Clawson. *Soil Conservation in Perspective.* Resources for the Future. Baltimore: John Hopkins University Press, 1965.

Howell, Glen. *CCC Boys Remember: A Pictoral History of the CCC.* Medford, Ore.: Klocker Printery, 1976.

Huxley, Julian. *TVA—Adventure in Planning.* Surrey, Eng.: Architectural Press, 1944.

Ickes, Harold L. *The Secret Diary of Harold L. Ickes.* Vol. 2, *The Inside Struggle, 1936–1939.* New York: Simon & Schuster, 1954.

Jolley, Harvey L. *The Blue Ridge Parkway.* Knoxville: University of Tennessee Press, 1969.

Kaufmann, Edgar and Ben Raeburn, eds. *Frank Lloyd Wright: Writings and Buildings.* Cleveland: World Publishing, 1965.

Kidney, Walter C. *The Architecture of Choice: Eclecticism in America, 1880–1930.* New York: George Braziller, 1974.

Kirkeminde, Patricia Barclay. *Cumberland Homesteads, As Viewed by the Newspapers* (Crossville, Tenn.: Brookhart Press, 1977).

Lilienthal, David. *TVA: Democracy on the March.* New York: Harper & Brothers, 1944.

Lowell, Guy, ed. *American Gardens.* Boston: Bates & Guild, 1902.

Merriam, Lewis. *Relief and Social Security.* Washington, D.C.: Brookings Institution, 1946.

National Recreation Association. *Standards in Playground Apparatus.* Washington, D.C.: NRA, 1929.

Naylor, Gillian. *The Arts and Crafts Movement.* Cambridge: MIT Press, 1971.

Nelson, Beatrice Ward. *State Recreation: Parks, Forests and Game Preserves.* Washington, D.C.: National Conference on State Parks, 1928.

Newton, Norman T. *Design on the Land: The Development of Landscape Architecture.* Cambridge: Harvard University Press, 1971.

Nixon, E. B., ed. *Franklin D. Roosevelt and Conservation, 1911–1945.* 2 vols. Washington, D.C.: GPO, 1957.

NPS. *Yearbook: Park and Recreation Progress.* 4 vols. Washington, D.C.: GPO, 1937–41.

_____. *A Study of the Park and Recreation Problem of the United States.* Washington, D.C.: GPO, 1941.

NPS and Emergency Relief Administration. *Park Use Studies and Demonstrations.* Washington, D.C.: GPO, 1941.

Platt, Charles. *Italian Gardens.* New York: Harper & Brothers, 1894.

_____. *Monograph of Charles A. Platt's Work.* New York: Architectural Book Publishing, 1913.

Pond, Bremer W. *Outline History of Landscape Architecture.* pts. 1, 2. Boston: Spalding-Moss, 1936.

Reps, John. *Monumental Washington: The Planning and Development of the Capitol Center.* Princeton: Princeton University Press, 1971.

Rose, Albert C. *Historic American Roads: From Frontier Trails to Superhighways.* New York: Crown Publishers, 1976.

Salmond, John A. *The Civilian Conservation Corps, 1933–1942: A New Deal Case Study.* Durham, N.C.: Duke University Press, 1967.

San Francisco, City of. *Fourth Annual Report of the Playground Commission.* 1911–12.

Schlesinger, Arthur M., Jr. *The Age of Roosevelt.* Vol. 1, *The Crisis of the Old Order, 1919–1933.* Vol. 2, *The Coming of the New Deal.* Vol. 3, *The Politics of Upheaval.* Boston: Houghton Mifflin, 1957–60.

Scott, Mel. *American City Planning since 1890.* Berkeley & Los Angeles: University of California Press, 1969.

Scully, Vincent J., Jr. *The Shingle Style and the Stick Style.* New Haven: Yale University Press, 1971.

Searle, Charles F. *Minister of Relief: Harry Hopkins and the Depression.* Syracuse, N.Y.: Syracuse University Press, 1963.

Shepherd, J. C. and G. A. Jellicoe. *Italian Gardens of the Renaissance.* New York: Charles Scribner & Sons, 1925.

Stein, Clarence S. *Toward New Towns for America.* New York: Reinhold Publishing, 1957.

Story, Isabelle F. *National Parks and Emergency Conservation.* Washington, D.C.: GPO, 1933.

Tilden, Freeman. *The State Parks: Their Meaning in American Life.* New York: Alfred A. Knopf, 1962.

TVA. Department of Regional Planning Studies. *Recreational Development of the Southern Highlands Region.* Knoxville, Tenn.: TVA, 1938.

Wattenberg, Ben J., ed. *Statistical History of the United States.* New York: Basic Books, 1976.

Weir, L. H., ed. *Parks: A Manual of Municipal and County Parks.* 2 vols. New York: A. S. Barnes, 1928.

Wharton, Edith. *Italian Villas and their Gardens.* London: J. Lane, 1904.

Whittick, Arnold, ed. *Encyclopedia of Urban Planning.* New York: McGraw-Hill, 1974.

Wirth, Conrad L. *Civilian Conservation Corps Program of the United States Department of the Interior.* Washington, D.C.: GPO, 1941.

Worster, Donald. *Dust Bowl: The Southern Plains in the 1930s.* New York: Oxford University Press, 1979.

Wright, Frank Lloyd. *Modern Architecture—Being the Kahn Lectures for 1930.* Princeton: Princeton University Press, 1931.

ARTICLES

Alexander, W. W. "The Rehabilitation and Tenancy Programs." *Soil Conservation* 4 (July 1938): 14–16.

Arrington, Leonard. "The New Deal in the West: A Preliminary Statistical Inquiry." *Pacific Historical Review* 38 (August 1969): 311–29.

Bennett, H. H. "Sunshine and Shadow." *Soil Conservation* 3 (August 1937): 30–33.

Berkeley, City of. *Civic Affairs*, 1933, 1934, 1940, 1941.

Bird, Jesse F. *Subsistence on the Small Farm with Special Reference to the Cumberland Plateau.* Bulletin #201. Knoxville: University of Tennessee Agricultural Experiment Station, 1946.

Borgeson, Melvin B. "Landscape Architect in Public Works: District One." *LA* 4 (October 1933): 27–28.

Bryan, Homer. "Oakland's Municipal Rose Garden." *Parks and Recreation* 19 (February 1936): 183–85.

"Buildings in the National Forest." *LA* 23 (July 1933): 263–64.

Carhart, Arthur H. "Landscape Architects and the One Hundred Fifty-Two National Forests." *LA* 11 (January 1921): 57–62.

Carnes, William G. "Landscape Architecture in the National Park Service." *LA* 41 (July 1951): 145–150.

Clarke, Gilmore D. "Notes on Texture in Stone Masonry." *LA* 21 (April 1931): 197–208.

Comptroller General of the United States. *Report to the Congress: Progress in Meeting Important Objectives of the Great Plains Conservation Program Could be Improved.* SCS. Washington, D.C.: GPO, 1973.

Cormier, Francis. "Some New York City Parks and Parkways: Recreational Development Made since 1934," *LA* 29 (April 1939): 124–36.

Cox, Laurie Davidson. "The Green Mountain Parkway." *LA* 25 (April 1935).

Draper, Earle S. "Levels of Planning." *Planners Journal* 3 (1937): 29–34.

_____. "Planning Methods in the Tennessee Valley." *American Civic Annual* 5 (1934): 110.

_____. "The Tennessee Valley Authority: The Landscape Architect in Public Works, part I." *LA* 24 (October 1933): 21–25.

Elwood, Philip H. "Some Landscape Architectural Problems in Government Service." *LA* 26 (July 1936): 189.

Federal Security Agency. *The CCC at Work*. Washington, D.C.: GPO, 1941.

"Forty Years with the SCS." *Soil Conservation* 40 (July 1975): 12–16.

Frincke, Harold C. "A New Regional Landscape: The Tennessee Valley Authority." In *Shaping Tomorrow's Landscape*, vol. 2. Edited by Sylvia Crowe and Zvi Miller. Djambatan: Publishers and Cartographers at Amsterdam, 1964.

Hamlin, Talbot F. "Farm Security Architecture: An Appraisal." *Pencil Points* 22 (November 1941): 709–20.

Hare, Herbert S. "The Municipal Rose Garden at Forth Worth." *Parks and Recreation* 17 (September 1933): 22–23.

Howard, Eugene A. "Recollections on Development of the Milwaukee County Park System." Unpublished Manuscript. Main office, Milwaukee County Park system, 1969.

"Ickes Would Keep Parks Natural." *American Forests* 41 (May 1935): 237.

Jennings, Allyn R. "Planning State Parks." *LA* 23 (July 1933): 221–34.

Keiley, James F. *A Brief History of the National Park Service.*

Koehler, Hans J. "Planting a Naturalistic Garden Theater in a Limestone Region." *LA* 14 (April 1924): 153–70.

Leopold, Aldo. "Coon Valley: An Adventure in Cooperative Conservation." *American Forests* 41 (May 1935): 205–08.

Lepawsky, Albert. "The Planning Apparatus: A Vignette of the New Deal." *Journal of the American Institute of Planners* 42 (January 1976): 16–32.

Livermore, Norman B. "Roads Running Wild." *American Forests* 44 (April 1938): 153–55.

Mayer, Albert. "The Greenbelt Towns Revisited." Parts 1–3. *Journal of Housing* 24 (January, February–March, April 1967).

Miller, E. Lynn. "Homesteading FDR-style at Arthurdale." *LA* 68 (September 1978): 418–23.

Morgan, Arthur E. "The Human Problem of the Tennessee Valley Authority." *LA* 24 (April 1934): 119–25.

Moses, Robert. "Municipal Recreation." *American Architect and Architecture* 149 (November 1936): 20–32.

Myrha, David. "Rexford Guy Tugwell: Initiator of America's Greenbelt New Towns, 1935–1936," *Journal of the American Institute of Planners* 40 (May 1974): 176–88.

Newton, Roger Hale. "Our Summer Resort Architecture—An American Phenomenon and Social Document." *Art Quarterly* 4 (Autumn 1941): 297.

"Pattern for Parks." *Architectural Forum* 65 (December 1936): 491–510.

Potter, Barrett G. "The 'Dirty Thirties' Shelterbelt Project." *American Forests* 82 (January 1976): 36–39.

Steiner, Jesse F. "America at Play: A Changing Panorama." *New York Times Magazine,* 2 July 1933.

————. "Challenge of the New Leisure." *New York Times Magazine,* 24 September 1933.

————. "Recreation and Leisure Time Activities." In President's Research Committee on Recent Social Trends, *Recent Social Trends in the United States* 2 (1933): 912–57.

Tabor, Paul and Arthur W. Susott. "Zero to Thirty Million Mile-a-Minute Seedlings." *Soil Conservation* 7 (September 1941): 61–65.

Taylor, A. D. "Notes on Federal Activities Relating to Landscape Architecture." *LA* 25–26 (January 1935–July 1936).

Tunnard, Christopher. "Modern Gardens for Modern Houses: Reflections on Current Trends in Landscape Design." *LA* 32 (January 1942): 57–68.

TVA. *A Short History of the Tennessee Valley Authority: 40th Anniversary of People in Partnership.* Knoxville, Tenn.: TVA, 1973.

"2,000,000,000 Seeds for Shelterbelt." *American Forests* 41 (May 1935): 249.

Urban, Abram Linwood. "The Seabrook Gardens: An Adaptation of Formal Gardening to Modern Living." *LA* 41 (January 1951): 49–56.

Vint, Thomas C. "National Park Service Master Plans." *Planning and Civic Comment* 12 (April 1946): 21–24.

Waugh, Frank A. "American Ideals in Landscape Architecture." *LA* 15 (April 1925): 151–54.

————. "Landscape Conservation: Planning the Recreational Use of Our Wild Lands." *Parks and Recreation* 19 (June 1936): 379–81.

————. *Landscape Engineering in the National Forest.* USFS, 1918.

GOVERNMENT DOCUMENTS AND PUBLICATIONS

Various government offices and archives and the heterogeneous holdings of the University of California at Berkeley provided me with my main sources of government documents and publications. The Government Documents section of U. C. Berkeley's Main Library offered up a good array of CCC promotional pamphlets: *The Civilian Conservation Corps and Public Recreation* (1941), *Reforestation by the CCC* (1938), and *Recreational Development by the CCC in National and State Forests* (1936) among others. Thanks to Charles Eliot, who closed up the National Resources Committee office, the Documents division also has numerous of that agency's pertinent publications. The historical Bancroft Library harbors two invaluable WPA summaries—*An Appraisal of the Results of the WPA* (1938) and *Summary Report on the Works Program in Northern California* (1938). True to character, the WPA did not record itself very well, but the School of Administration at Harvard did yield a *Final Report on the WPA, 1935–1943* (1946), and other more specific publications concerning that agency. U. C. Berkeley's Agricultural Library shelters information on the soil conservation effort, while TVA forestry information came in part from the Forestry Library. The Environmental Design Library abounds in the period's rich harvest of recreational publications, as well as a tantalizing supply of background twenties and thirties landscape readings.

Gleanings from federal sources were highly unpredictable, sometimes surprisingly fine through beneficial neglect. The USFS San Francisco office hosted an invaluable collection of old National Recreation Association publications until some well-intended individual updated the collection. The National Park Service Western Regional Office in San Francisco offered up a full set of NPS *Annual Reports* and the highly useful NPS *Yearbook(s): Park and Recreation Progress* for the years 1937–1941. As for first-hand, on-site reporting, the different West Coast national parks kept copious records with occasional glints of interest that are stored at the Federal Records Center in San Bruno, California. The Technical Library at Knoxville houses the extensive self-documentation of the TVA.

Cities keep their records with widely varying degrees of conscientiousness. Philadelphia, Dallas, and the Cleveland Metropolitan Park District did the best job; Chicago and Berkeley kept good records then lost some. New York's *Six Years* (1940) *Eight Years* (1942) and *Twenty Years of Park Progress* (1969), like their initiator Robert Moses, are highly personalized, idiosyncratic, and fascinating. San Francisco never got beyond its Park Commission minutes. As for Boston's records, like its works program, *something happened.* The conclusion on primary documents is that they aren't always where you expect them.

Index